The Silent Killer of Police & First Responders

Building Endurance to Manage the Effects of Accumulated Stress, Adversity & Trauma

Assisting Self & Helping Others
Practical Applications of Research and Practice

By

Richard C. Lumb, Ph.D.

ISBN-10: 1492114618
ISBN-13: 978-1492114611
BISAC: Education / Counseling / General
All Rights Reserved.
Wilton, ME., PSPP&R

Lumb, R., & Rogers, J. (2013). *No Excuses Supervision: Role Changes to Reflect 21st Century Demands.* ISBN-10: 1493654373 ISBN-13: 978-1493654376, Amazon Publishing.

Lumb, R., & Lumb, P. (2014). *The Silent Killer of Police & First Responders* ISBN-10: 1492114618 Amazon Publishing

Breazeale, R., & Lumb, R. (2013). *Resilience Building: Peer Coaching.* ISBN-10: 1492812447 ISBN-13: 978-1492812449. Amazon Publishing.

Lumb, R. (2014) *25 Assertions About Leader* Roles and Effectiveness ISBN-13: 978-1500752316 Amazon Publishing

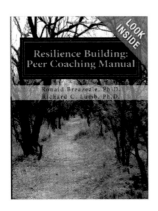

Concerns and Focus of the Manuscript.

Police, Corrections, Fire, EMS and other police and first responders' encounter danger, adversity, stress and trauma (SAT) throughout their career. The negative long-term psychological, emotional, physiological and social impact of SAT all too often ends in tragedy.

www2.alcatel-lucent.com

Organizations provide all manner of body protection that include bullet resistance vests, weapons, chemical sprays, breathing apparatus, protective suits and other equipment to keep the officer's physical body safe. However, the emotional and psychological well-being is left to the individual and the results are abysmal.

Understanding and addressing emotional and psychological manifestations, using proven methods and techniques to strengthen personal resilience and grit, is long overdue.

The Silent Killer of Police and First Responders

Building Endurance to Manage the Effects of Accumulated Stress, Adversity & Trauma [ASAT]

Content

About the Author

Richard C. Lumb, PhD, received his doctorate from Florida State University and is an Emeritus Associate Professor and Chair of the Department of Criminal Justice, the State University of New York at Brockport. He was an Associate Professor at the University of North Carolina at Charlotte and Northern Michigan University where he also served as graduate coordinator in the Criminal Justice Department. He also served as Chair of the Criminal Justice Department at Western Piedmont Community College, Morganton, NC. WPCC was a certified Basic Law Enforcement Training site and in-service training provider for Western North Carolina. He currently is an Adjunct Professor at the University of Maine at Augusta, University of Massachusetts at Lowell and the University of Massachusetts at Boston.

He completed twenty-four years of policing serving with the Maine State Police and as a Chief of Police in two departments. Lumb served as Director of the Research, Planning and Analysis Bureau for the Charlotte-Mecklenburg Police Department that included Project Director of the Carolinas Institute for Community Policing in North and South Carolina. CMPD converted from traditional to community problem oriented policing in that period of time.

Utilizing his Public Safety Planning, Policy & Research L.L.C., and Maine Woods Education & Training Services component, he is engaged in consultation, program development, delivery and evaluation, specialized program assessment, and engages in research and publication on a variety of topics. For the past five years, Lumb has been engaged in the delivery of programs on personal resilience and endurance building. Resilience education and training is designed to meet the needs of organizations and individuals who may encounter adversity, stress, traumatic and life changing events. This training adopts a prevention and pre-event focus, teaching people responses to traumatic events, thereby reducing the impact and allowing responses that overcome debilitation. The program also teaches people to appropriately handle personal, home, work and community related events that traumatize, may be life threatening and contribute to fear and discouragement. The ability to endure, to react with confidence, and to effectively continue on while others are incapacitated emerges from personal resilience.

Teaching peer coaches to reach out to help others in their organization is critical. The decision to engage, to do so with clear intent, knowledgeable applications, and sincerity and concern for the other person, improves lives, and removes the ghosts that can plague us. It is not just an emergency room endeavor, rather it is personal, where caring and willingness to help another person shines brightly through the gloom of discouragement and despondence.

These past ten years, the resilience program was delivered to police, sheriff, fire, corrections and EMT personnel. Peer coaching resilience training for public safety and first responder personnel is one of the primary focus areas, providing skills to help manage crisis, reduce everyday stressful situations, and being more effective in meeting job and personal demands that are associated with everyday living. Lumb remains active in sustainable community capacity building as it relates to quality of life issues and needs, helping agencies and communities find solutions to long-term and vexing problems.

Acknowledgements

This book would not be possible were it not for the contribution, understanding, patience and encouragement of my wife, Paula. These factors were the fuel that kept me on track. She saw the concern I feel for the men and women who wear the uniform and perform the tough duties for the well-being of their fellow citizens. We know and recognize that change can take place with agencies providing the same protection to the emotional and psychological aspects of our first responders, as we do for protection against physical harm. The clear answer is, absolutely!

A partial list of these individuals include Police, Fire, Corrections, Emergency Medical & Paramedics, Game Wardens, Emergency Management, 911 Telecommunications Personnel, Hazmat, Search & Rescue, Public Health Services, Sea & Shore Fisheries, Wildlife Officers, Rangers, Coast Guard, Military Personnel, Crisis Intervention, Mental Health, and others who respond to situations of potential harm and hazard.

As with any endeavor in life, successful outcomes are more likely when we work with others. The drive behind this book emerges from my life's work with police, first responders and other services in both criminal justice and public safety; spanning over fifty years, twenty-four of them in police agencies.

The job responsibilities fulfilled by Police, Corrections, Fire Fighters, EMTs, Game Wardens, Sea and Shore Fisheries, Forest Wardens, Court Services, Probation and Parole, Emergency Management, Capitol Police and others from municipal, county, state and federal agencies, address issues, problems, needs and all manner of trauma that others prefer to avoid. The outcome of these encounters can cause elevated stress, adversity and trauma. Over time there is an accumulation of stress takes its toll, leaving behind damaging residue that impacts the psychological, physiological, emotional and social aspects of the life of the individual. The spill-over also impacts on the individual's family, friends, colleagues and other relationships.

Police and First Responders that I have known number in the hundreds. All do their work in a competent and professional manner and deserve the public's support and celebration. Those that stand out in their field and understand the issues and work to address them, include the following individuals. I wish to acknowledge their continuing contribution to the health and well-being of employees and others who currently or previously work in public safety.

- Ronald L. Breazeale, Ph.D., Clinical Psychologist, Portland, Maine
- Jerry DeWitt, LSW, Tri-County Mental Health Services. A military veteran who devotes his life to the issues and needs of veterans and their families.
- Sheriff Kevin Joyce, Cumberland County Maine, Office of the Sheriff
- Chief Dana Kelley, Old Orchard Beach Maine Police Department
- Sheriff Randall Liberty, Kennebec County Maine, Office of the Sheriff
- Associate Professor Gary Metz, State University of New York at Brockport
- Chief Ken Miller, Greenville, SC Police Department
- Chief Robert Moulton, Scarborough Maine Police Department
- Chief Michael Thurlow, Scarborough Maine Fire Department

The faces of police and first responders provide a window to the internal world of their feelings and emotions. When encountering the adversity or exposure to danger, trauma, and other negative job related events, they present a mask of determination, strength and fortitude. They face their duties without complaint knowing that what they do provides for the greater good.

An event that has summoned an officer or public safety response must now be handled, take charge, and bring order to disorder. They confront danger and endure as a silent witness to yet another human tragedy. No tears will fall, no emotion witnessed, and the physiological and psychological systems of the officer will instantly achieve full power as anticipation, safety, and decisions are made at light speed.

A state of high readiness is taking place, automatic and in response to perceived danger. The officer's focus is acute as he or she scans and processes what is observed and a rise in protective action from potential danger peaks instantly. They develop a response to the issue or emergency that they cannot avoid.

The officer's senses are sharpened, eyes rapidly observing, smells and sounds are more acute, and the movement and behavior of people observed are mentally acknowledged. The officer's adrenal gland releases adrenalin resulting in an increased heart rate, a flaring of nasal passages for the intake of additional oxygen, eye pupils enlarge and the individual's muscles receive more blood in anticipation of increased body activity. Elevated adrenaline is necessary when facing danger or high intensity situations, but when accumulated in the bloodstream, it has harmful consequences that lead to insomnia, nervousness, and lower immunity. Considering the number of high stress situations in one's career, there are concerns for the officer's health over time.

One incident becomes hundreds or thousands with the passing of years. Each event carries a level of stress and adversity and it adversely impacts on the individual's health and well-being. The normal approach to self-management of uncomfortable feelings is to suck it up, move forward, and deal with it. To some, it may lead to increased alcohol and/or drug use, and other potentially injurious behavior. We should establish a positive goal of increasing the person's life balance. Negative encounters elevate stress and also impacts on family, peers and others in one's life. If the effects of stress and adversity are making themselves known in uncomfortable and negative ways, do we not have an obligation to address them?

We outfit our personnel with all manner of safety equipment and tools of the craft; we do little to safeguard the emotional, psychological and social aspects, which, when confronting the effects of accumulated stress and adversity, simply pay the price for the absence of equal protection. Denial obscures facing reality and relieves having to address the issues and take action to fix them. This condition is all too common, but the good news is, it can be managed. But first there must be the inclination and commitment to do so.

In the officer's head, the neurons that connect the prefrontal lobes of the brain, resting just behind the forehead, are surging tides of thought and feelings that blast forth into consciousness. The intellect, located in the neocortex a more recently evolved layer at the top of the brain, is making contact with the ancient subcortex, located lower and deeper in the brain. The reception and processing of information leads to decisions and evokes emotional response. In an emerging dangerous situation, where harm or death could result, the biological fight or flight syndrome flashes red, signaling the need for action by the individual and adrenalin surges giving the person extreme energy and awareness. The emotion of fear elicits caution and awareness. Feelings of happiness, comfort and other thoughts are shut down due to the heightened awareness of unusualness and the need for full attention to what is being confronted.

Facial expressions, voice pitch and tone, body language and other perceptible manifestations indicate the need to control, to take charge, and to bring order to chaos. The officer's sweat glands are over producing. His or her heart is beating faster and more rapid and shallow breaths are being taken as the stress of the moment maintains heightened awareness and a sense of protection, warning, and potential for danger. The officer's training kicks in and many automatic reactions will occur – all within the proper bounds of what has been instilled into a response being determined.

And, when it is over, bodily functions seek to return to normal. There is often a feeling of fatigue, sometimes disbelief, anger, hunger and the need to be around others who can understand what was just experienced. When officers have gathered to sit and wind down at the end of high stress events, they often resort to retelling the stories of what just happened. They emphasize thrilling events, points of danger, observations and feelings toughened by exposure, often these retellings are laced with descriptions of perps as "assholes" and other descriptives that indicate the distain and revulsion they are feeling. Reliving and reviewing the event helps with their understanding of what remains a blurry event. It is not simple complaining; it is a stress reliever, tension reducing process. From a physical system that ramped up to meet the threat with additional adrenalin, faster heartbeat, rapid breathing, tense muscles, and physiological enhancements needed as the person addressed risk and potential danger, it is greatly needed.

Group discussion helps to reduce stress and elicit support from others. This activity, like a pressure cooker release valve, allows the internal heightened emotions to slowly return to normal. It is at this moment that the officer is very aware of feelings that will range from the need to cry to extreme exhilaration and real or feigned anger. On occasion, the officer or group will retire to a local bar of choice where the stories are retold along with consumption of alcohol, the medication of choice for some. A spouse or other family member, who are part of the officer's life, will typically not be present for these events. Not sharing gives both parties reason to distance themselves from one another. Often this is not done consciously. But it effectively builds barriers that are difficult to surmount. The gap tends to grow, spreading outward in gradual decay until the individual finds the chasm too wide to cross anymore.

A freight-train of emotion occurred and it took away a substantial piece of normalcy. Left in its wake is a subtle layer of stress that will not diminish by itself. As time passes and numerous similar situations occur, the layers deepen and the trauma encountered increases damage. We often see the results manifesting themselves in harmful ways. When compared with the normal population, police and first responders experience a higher rate of heart ailment, obesity, excessive use of alcohol or drugs, relationship problems, and social atrophy. In addition, there are elevated levels of anger and distrust that rule the head and heart. Clearly, none of this is healthy (Williams and Huber, 1986).

The employing organization provides the physical body with protection from harm with vests, guns, pepper spray, handcuffs and other equipment. Yet, rarely is there a career long plan to address the emotional or cognitive side. The long term outcome of this neglect is often reflected by higher than normal early deaths, suicide, physical and mental illness – signs of deterioration from a lifetime of traumatic encounters that were not properly addressed. There is a withering of life that has stripped away any chance for healthy longevity in a post career lifestyle.

Core problematic issues begin long before an incident occurred and no intervention was taken to head off future employee dysfunction.

One of my passions is to address the extent to which stress, adversity and trauma (S.A.T.) impacts the lives of police officers and first responders. Stress and adversity are more subtle, as over time, both wreak havoc on the individual and the lingering effects are cumulative. A traumatic event is often sudden with accompanying negative experiences, all of which are harmful.

Often employee aberrant behavior results in discipline and less frequently, dismissal or conviction. We begin examination of bad behavior at the point of occurrence. In reality, the core issues began long before and no one stepped into the breach and made the appropriate corrections or provided direction to establish sustainable change. "Kicking ass" and "ordering" someone to shape up may work in boot camp, but not so well in the adult professional life of our employees.

Summary

The effects of stress are gradual and when yet another traumatic event occurs, adopting a supervisory attitude of "suck it up," masks the need to be serious in how we address the issue. Toughening it out, sure, it [seems] to work for many. But the underlying issue continues to eat away at the person and soon relief for the uncomfortable feelings, anger, frustration and other affective manifestations are soothed with alcohol, drugs, promiscuity, overt behavior (walking the razors edge) and other behaviors that are not healthy are adopted to help the person feel better. Domestic and family issues worsen, odd behavior is observed and yet, silence from peers and supervisors, until the crowning event, the incident, from which some never recover.

PART I: Dangers of the Job: Unprotected by Body Armor

Chapter 1
The Academy: It Begins There

The decision to seek employment in public safety or a first responder occupation generally follows personal hunch and intuition, a sense that you would like that type of work and want to give it a try. It may emerge from having a family member in a similar occupation, a favorite TV show, personal observation, school resource officer contact or another external influence. It is a strong interest with motivation to seek a job that is reinforced by an emerging commitment, that propels one forward to determine more information and what next steps to take in pursuit of such a career.

Generally, the image of what the job entails is unrealistic, as experience is a missing factor that may moderate later enthusiasm. Following time in an occupation, sometimes will lead the individual to resign and seek other occupational pursuits. It is not possible to know all of the positive and negative aspects of an unknown career path until one 'jumps in.' Outside views are often masked by real and modified behavior guided by rule of law, organizational policy and oversight by supervisors. The reality of working in a public safety role accumulates gradually, incident by incident, as well as through exposure to all manner of experience the job presents. While there are many positives, there are also many very traumatic and negative incidents, as that is the nature of the job.

Overtime, the Academy experience elevates how the former civilian, and now emerging first responder, feels and thinks. His or her behavior and attitude and gradual alteration in and social functioning takes place. Given the nature of the profession these internal and external changes and responses cannot be avoided. Dispatch directs where the individual goes and the expectation is to respond. Thus, exposure to this profession impacts the individual in both positive and negative ways. The residue is not shed at the door when going off duty. It is this very residue that concerns us, for it can be, and often is, harmful and even deadly.

I. What Individuals Bring to the Academy?

<u>Family, Friends, School and Other Influences.</u>

The first thought of job interest becomes a process where inquiry and planning take place, eventually leading to potential employment. The process is lengthy and inquiry into every aspect of the applicant's life is explored and questioned. Physical, emotional, social, and financial well-being is examined. At any stage of the process, discovery of issues that challenge "fit" to the job may be uncovered and the process can come to a halt.

When the decision is made to apply, family members are told and reconciliation and acceptance by those closest to the applicant are undertaken. Not all family members or loved ones may be enthusiastic, but generally objections are not raised, at least to the level of forcing a halt to the quest for occupational admittance. Still, there are questions that must be answered, for to not do so will have later consequences. Often insufficient time is taken in making the decision. When the application is submitted, the department is often an absent partner as the process slowly unfolds. At each milestone the applicant is informed of the outcome and the wait begins again.

It is recommended that the department spend upfront time to provide in-depth information of what will take place, a timetable, and provide answers to earlier questions posed by those other applicants come came before them. Full information is necessary to allow for good decision-making. All parties are better served when the decision to apply is made with full knowledge of what can be expected and why. Processing a police and first responder candidate is expensive and demands extensive resource time. Therefore it makes sense to align all parties to the process, if for no other reason than efficiency.

Preparing for a Cultural and Belief Shift.

The philosophy and beliefs that you bring to the training academy will change over time. Most academies follow the semi-military model, meaning there are demands for compliance to orders and instructions, learning formations, understanding rank, personal behavior expectations and rules, to name a few. There is generally a degree of "in your face" by academy cadre that teaches tolerance, patience, self-discipline and other skills and attitudes that will be helpful when the job begins in earnest. You begin to see and hear references to safety, survival and duty. You learn that when all others are running from danger, you are racing toward it. You are introduced to strategies and techniques that can protect you from harm and also hear that injury and death sometimes occur when carrying out your duties.

Some of your peers, and certainly others who come to the Academy to teach or to provide other support, will use language that is shocking, as it is not uncommon to hear people referred to as "assholes" or "scum bags" and other derogatory descriptives. Questions about issues and trust of people outside the profession elicit statements of mistrust, question and stories on how no one should be under-estimated. As you mull this over, your former trust level is slipping, even as you wonder if it can be true...it must be true or why would these experienced instructors say it? As your view of the public begins to shift and emphasis is placed on the types of issues you will encounter, it may seem that the world is descending into chaos. The job you are seeking to achieve has enormous implications. The separation from what you knew has begun and the path to a new sub-culture is underway.

II. Influence of the Academy Role and Culture.

What the Academy's Role is all About?

Converting a person from a civilian role to one where they become society's hall monitor and subjected to all manner of conflict, trauma and regulatory responsibility takes time, skill building and attitude change. Strangers become a team and work collaboratively in bringing themselves to a level of proficiency that is established by rigid academy rules and policy. Transferring earlier attitudes and beliefs to a new focus, where they separate themselves from what they knew, to what they will become, is a necessary process. It is also a stressful process and one where persistence and grit are called for. Any less will result in not making the grade and being dismissed from the quest. This is how it should be, for unless the recruit has total commitment and willingness to endure the rigors of the job, it will be a long and trying career, one that will end voluntarily or otherwise, perhaps sooner than later.

Compliance and Adaptation.

The process of becoming a professional requires a willingness to take instruction, to follow orders and to perform at one's top level of expertise and motivation. It is not possible to fake one's way through the rigors of academy training as there are multiple opportunities to measure compliance and observe performance. Academy staff demand 100 percent effort and the rationale for that goal is borne in the realities of the job.

Job reality takes time to acquire. Experience and exposure to situations and people, along with the accompanying baggage, can change one's perspective over time.

The known becomes unknown and in that venue, we begin to see the world in a different light!

Every academy class feels their training was more harsh and demanding than those that preceded and followed what they went through. The truth is, each individual approaches the experience with a variety of expectations and beliefs coupled with fortitude and determination. The level of difficulty is often viewed from within the experience and less from what is expected. Stress applied to the training seeks to cut loose those who cannot manage it or who find it contrary to what was expected. Leaving is not to be considered as "the individual cannot take it" rather we all respond to challenges and confrontation in different ways and decisions that are forthcoming should be respected.

Formations, teamwork, academic challenge, skill development and level of compliance are geared to effective outcomes. When the future officer or agent confronts situations that are potentially dangerous, demand control, and are a challenge to citizens who cannot manage what is taking place; proficiency is all important. First responders often encounter situations where the general public is unable to manage and control events. Managing a situation is often a challenge and demands careful attention. Academy training can replicate those situations and provide the guidance needed to return the situation to a balanced state of being.

Public respect is one of the goals to be learned. Responders are taught to listen, to weigh what is heard and to seek truth in what is observed. It is not possible to satisfy every person in each situation and conflict may arise. Training instructs the individual on how to mediate and retain control in the face of adversity.

Consider Personal Vision, Values and Beliefs: Reconciling Differences

The path to a full career is highly dependent on the outlook the individual has about the role he or she will play and the manner in which they perceive their roles in a democratic society. You will soon face varying opinions of other employees and they

14

should not be taken as gospel! Each individual deals with exposure to the dangers, inhumanity, the comedy, joy, sadness, humility, bizarre and unfathomable behaviors that will be observed and require intervention. Form your own opinions, take steps to manage how you will act, react and behave in situations, for the ultimate accountability falls squarely on your shoulders.

You have to learn to co-exist with others and become part of a tight-knit culture. But you must not abdicate your "self" for the group, especially when the direction is or feels wrong. It is always healthy to review your personal vision of how to do the job, what your values are with respect to dealing with people and situations that represent how you perform your duties. Any personal mission must blend with that of the organization. When a personal mission and the organization's mission are in conflict, job performance is not balanced and steps must be taken to resolve the issue. Your beliefs will change and it will be easy to fall into the conviction that everyone is an "asshole." Eventually you will realize they are not and you will learn who to trust as your personal confidence grows.

III. What to Take into the Field.

Graduation is a Beginning to Decades of Change.

The person who entered basic training emerges in a different place mentally, physically and philosophically. Gone is the care-free soul, for you have learned to follow orders, to reach deep into your personal level of grit and to learn numerous new skills whose application may reflect life and death. Consider how you thought about the issues you are told will be yours to address. Consider some of the scenarios, photographs, videos and stories seen and heard and compare that with the general population. Is it any wonder people do not understand? But, most of this is in a protective environment where safeguards are in place to prevent your injury and well-being.

No such protection can be 100 percent at the street level when seconds coalesce into micro-seconds and choices that you make must be a reflex, automatic and right the first time out.

You are about to enter the next phase of the job and acquire a new set of change perspectives. The street awaits you.

The world of public safety service. Citizens and the Weight of the Agency.

The people you encounter will be thankful you have arrived, worried about what you will do and may not like you for what you represent. Then, there are always the observers, those who gawk and get in the way. Some are friendly, some are dangerous and others bear watching, as it is difficult to place them in any category, until more time is spent in their presence. In all instances, you must be aware of your environment, what is going on around you, looking for the small indicators that something has changed, requiring heightened awareness and attention, for it relates directly to safety. If you "feel" something is not right, it probably isn't. Pay attention, be observant, and be safe as you are your own first line of defense.

You will learn to control your emotions, to be rigid and not think about the child that has been scorched by the live-in boyfriend's cigarette. But, even though the conscious images can be forced from your presence, they linger and burrow in to reemerge again and again. If not managed properly the effects of stress, adversity and trauma will affect your mental and physical health, your social relationships, and it can wreak havoc with your emotions. For example, police and first responder departments supply all manner of protective gear to minimize and prevent injury of the body and do little to address the psychological and emotional aspects.

Therein lays a trap door, one that is often hidden to you but observable to others, who learn how to <u>not</u> say or do things that will cause a negative response. Exacerbated by stress and a narrowing of patience, understanding and willingness to find middle ground diminishes over time. What replaces it is a hardening of attitude, a narrowing perspective, a more cautious demeanor, less trust, and increasing frustration and anger with situations you cannot change.

Chapter 2
The Journey to Perdition:
Accumulated Job Related Stress and Adversity

The Nature of Stress and Adversity.

Human beings have undergone millennium of evolution, learning survival skills, and living in groups for mutual protection. This has created the most successful species on the planet and aided in fulfilling our basic needs of shelter, food, and sharing in the process of daily life.

As society evolved the decision was made to hire others to provide protection, respond and to conduct investigation into offenses that the social group experienced. In other words, we created a response system to address society's needs. With the passage of time the role of first responder evolved into a presence that is accessible to all citizens by placing a simple telephone call. Our police, fire fighters, correctional staff, game wardens, EMTs, Coast Guard and many other first responders who man the front lines, 365 days a year, stand tall and are ready to provide their expertise to a demanding public. It is that single call, repeated thousands of times daily that eventually lead to an overwhelming residue of trauma resulting in physical, emotional and social damage to those who must answer the demand for help. Subtle nicks in the psychological armor, over time, leave it threadbare or at the end of the career simply tear it apart, leaving the one time protections in tatters.

Bear in mind that these occupations engage in events that the general population shuns or flees from. Consider corrections staff and the daily encounter with inmate issues and problems. Constantly being on-guard against assault and injury, maintaining order, and long periods of hypervigilance take a toll on the emotional and physical health of individuals. And, other correctional program and support staffs, medical, dental and administrative personnel experience a fair share of stress. The anxiety of emergency medical service professionals is another group that will experience the silent killer of stress to a larger degree than the general public. All manner of human harm is encountered and must be reacted to, fast and in a professional manner. These same circumstances are faced by other emergency and enforcement personnel, but fortunately with appropriate training to manage the situation.

Issues and events that affect well-being, health, relationships, work, and other circumstances associated with daily life occur and when they do our reaction assumes many responses. A sudden automobile accident, injury, family crisis, work disruption, national emergency, a traumatic and chaotic event that is manmade or environmental disaster can present a challenge that did not exist just moments before. Our reactions take many forms when a traumatic event is experienced. This may include disbelief, the need to escape/flee, become immobilized or the inability to react out of fear and shock. These are automatic responses that represent experience, prior learning and training, as well as survival instinct. When normalcy and routine are disrupted by a

17

higher level of trauma or chaos it takes time to mentally process information and formulate a response[1].

The Dartmouth College Health Service, Counseling and Human Development Department listed the following potential individual responses to encountering a traumatic event[2]. Consider these many reactions:

- Denial, shock, numbness
- Feeling vulnerable, unsafe
- Anxiety, panic, worry
- Irritability, anger, moodiness
- Being hyper-alert or vigilant
- Disturbing images
- Headaches, fatigue, sleep disturbances
- Helplessness, hopelessness
- Sadness, crying, despair
- Difficulty concentrating
- Withdrawal, isolation
- Remembering other life traumas
- Confusion, forgetfulness, or memory impairment
- Use of alcohol or other substances to cope with disturbing feelings
- Often, we have no reaction at all.

The silent killer waits with patience until sufficient pressure builds and relief is not within safe limits; rather it is often found in the use of substances or behavior so out of character that recovery is in danger of being excluded and permanent harm is the outcome.

If multiple people are involved in the same incident and experiencing the same conditions, mass hysteria or panic is a potential outcome. Restoration of order becomes difficult, if the event is of long duration, as conditions and responses are exacerbated to crisis levels. Many of the above responses to a traumatic event also manifest themselves with long-term exposure to adversity, crisis, and disaster response associated with work and professional duty. The point being, experiencing abnormal and unusual events that require high levels of unnatural response can be detrimental to a person's health and result in dysfunction, disability, and even death.

Of course, not everyone emerges with issues, but when we examine police suicide and divorce it is higher than the normal population. Retired police, correctional

---

[1]. From a forthcoming document by Richard Lumb. A prevention model to strengthen individual and community resilience: Diminishing the effects of crisis, adversity and trauma.
[2]. http://www.dartmouth.edu/~chd/resources/tragedy/index.html

officers and other public safety personnel experience early death due to heart, respiratory and other physical ailments. Those groups experience substance abuse, smoking, and other lifestyle issues in an attempt to lessen the discomfort they feel in every waking moment. They worry about vulnerability and security, exhibit hypervigilance, and remain on-guard against phantom assailants when in public. The stress and adversity encountered often goes unnoticed and is a silent threat. It is quite serious if left unattended over a twenty-five year career. The silent killer wreaks havoc on family and peers and others with whom he or she associates, as well.

Brian's Story

This is Brian's story. Yet, it portrays each of us who ever worked in police and first responder services or provided emergency services to public needs. The story is the genesis of this book, a tale of joy, heartbreak and tragedy. It tells of moments of exhilaration that are unrivaled by other events except the experience of war or the terror encountered by a victim of senseless violence and despicable acts. Brian is a police officer but he also represents other specialty groups that include Corrections, Fire and EMS, Emergency Management, FEMA, Military, Environmental, Hazardous Materials and other emergency response agencies.

Upon meeting Brian, you would encounter someone who portrays a variety of personalities, representative of others in this occupational field. There is also the inner self who occasionally wrestles with demons, harbors anger and suspicion, acts with caution, complains about justice, is judgmental and generally unsettled. Brian's friendships are mostly tied to the job. They are not of instant acquisition and typically take time to build trust and acceptance.

Years of negative encounters with people eventually exacted a toll on Brian's emotions and physical well-being. Many officers have learned the lesson that to trust a stranger is to invite trouble. Therefore, the first impression is sometimes replaced with negative reality. Brian, and others like him, encounters many people while on-duty who appear normal. However, upon closer inspection, he found them to be narcissistic, predatory, untrustworthy, and with a hidden side that obscures images of right from wrong.

Brian considered the changes in his life, looking back at the first ten years in uniform. He felt the raw resentment rising in his chest. The feelings of frustration that were making themselves felt with noticeable discomfort. Restlessness was ever-present. Brian often had the urge to swear at unseen ghosts that torment in the night, interrupting sleep and leaving him feeling disoriented in the morning. His first thought was to seek comfort in the job from peers and the few who were closest to him; other police officers. These were the people he could trust and in whose presence he felt most comfortable.

He was in his kitchen drinking coffee and feeling lonely. This was not the loneliness that comes from being alone. Rather, this solitude was the realization that unless he was on-duty, in uniform and in contact with others working the same shift, he felt out of place. Comfort was wearing a gun, badge and the knowledge you were different from the rest of society. Off-duty, the ever present concealed weapon and identification carried everywhere brought comfort and, if needed, he could immediately establish who he was. Identifying oneself as a police officer brought immediate reaction from people and the general response was one of recognition and respect, even from bad guys. Vulnerability was of major concern and not being prepared to confront danger or a situation where harm may be encountered was constantly on his mind. How many bad guys had he locked up? How often had Brian been in moderate to severe confrontation? Those who would strike at him in an instant if they felt they had the advantage? No, being strong and being prepared was the only path to follow. The problem, how to accomplish that?

<u>Aspects of stress that no one talks about.</u>

Stress and adversity form a partnership that attack a person's health, physical and emotional well-being. It is not generally a fast acting influence. It accumulates over time and layer upon layer builds in negative ways that are harmful. Public safety and first responder work is widespread with stress-related engagements that include the nature of the job itself, organizational practices, the public and the justice system (Reece, 1986). And, there is the element of ever present danger of harm, injury and death.

A common complaint is the lack of support by administration, the focus is perceived as being on policy and not personnel. Discipline and punishment are the main response to complaints and numerous other internal and external influences. Complaints about the promotional process, the feeling they are guilty and must prove themselves innocent, political influence and the semi-military nature of the job that puts rank before competence, at times. And, while there is often enormous discretion, they often complain about being second-guessed by administration, courts, public opinion and media scrutiny.

The complexity of managing a police or other first responder and public safety agency is well known. A common complaint today is a real or perceived separation of administration from the rank and file.

Corrections staff are also under many points of stress. Beyond the obvious peril of assault, there are other factors that form many thin layers of anxiety. Corrections staff are scrutinized by the public and the media. Many offenders with an axe to grind concoct horrible allegations against staff. These factors, over time, like the slow and steady formation of the sedimentary layers of the Grand Canyon, create complex layers of tension.

A daily routine interrupted by any one of the listed causes of stress brings immediate negative response and concern for being singled out. Reaching out to the Union representative or other association sometimes allows the protective wall to slam shut as the officer takes refuge within. Polarization expands and the process of "point and counter point" begins. The effect on service, performance and attitude suffers. The fear of external intervention or oversight is paralyzing. It creates an agency against itself mentality. Self-policing results and all manner of separation and division among employees occurs when internal tensions over-ride focus on mission and goals the organization is less effective and efficient and does a disservice to the client.

There are other forces impacting on the organization and employees, shift work notwithstanding, such as encounters with deviance, danger, boredom and ever present social flux. The totality of these pressures weaves in and out of an officer's life and eventually strikes a blow to health, emotions and relationships. It seems unavoidable. Sadly, even in the 21st Century we do not address the issues from an organizational perspective (with some exceptions) leaving the officer to his or her own endeavors to find a solution to what may be or has become a serious problem.

A study by Millson (2009) shows the various causes of correctional officer stress.

Table 1[3]
Causes of stress for correctional officers

External organizational factors	Internal Organizational factors
• Public's view of correctional officers	• Understaffing
• Level of pay	• Overtime
• Work environment	• Management support
• Dangerousness	• Career progression
• Inmate interactions	• Communication and decision-making
• Boredom	• Role conflict and ambiguity
• Problems with co-workers	• Attitudes toward correctional
• Demographic factors work	• Correctional Orientation
• Gender	• Job Satisfaction
• Education	
• Correctional experience	

How many of the variables listed are being addressed with carefully conscripted programs designed to reduce the level of pressure and stress? Generally, when any one of them erupts into a problem, it is dealt with using discipline, a reactive response.

Early manifestations of stress include an increasing negative attitude. It becomes commonplace to complain about all manner of things, from schedules, to supervisors, to Judges, to a system that is too liberal, to the need for someone to get tough on criminals etc. Life becomes a giant complaint session. Belief systems suffer in a corresponding manner, leaving the individual with a negative outlook about the job, and feeling unhappy. Granted, there may be some therapeutic value to complaining as it tends to soften weighty issues and generally attracts others of like

---

[3]. Millson, William. (2009). Predictors of work stress among correctional officers. Master thesis, Carleton University. Correctional Service of Canada. http://www.csc-scc.gc.ca/text/pblct/forum/e141/e141l-eng.shtml

mind who commiserate. Misery loves company. It is not difficult to assemble like-minded people who agree that the world is going to hell in a hand basket. Often a complaint, raised by an individual, becomes the group issue as discussion and justification is passed from person to person.

On a daily basis, first responders encounter levels of stress and adversity that places them at significantly higher risk than the general population. Stress is not generally a sudden manifestation whose symptoms suddenly explode; there are more subtle indicators that include sleeplessness, obesity, hypertension, anger, intolerance, hyper-vigilance and other symptoms. And perhaps the most alarming statistic is that a study[4] conducted in Buffalo, New York (2012) indicated that suicide rates were eight times higher in working police officers than those who left the force or retired.

Victims.

Certainly the first responder becomes a victim. But unless they live in a vacuum, other people in their life also suffer. Spouses and children are often left in a state of confusion as to why their loved one is grumpy much of the time and why they often are harsh in dealing with home and family issues. There is an overly controlling side that emerges whenever the family member is going to be in public. Protection and over concern for safety leads to questions about whom their child associates with or where they are going. There is worry and fear that something horrible will happen. This opens the need to be over-protective. In doing so, over-zealous behavior surfaces and all manner of caution, harsh rules and threats emerge, leaving the recipient feeling hurt and angry. Family life takes the hit due to officer caution, depression, anger and fear of the unknown coupled with a deep need to control. What emerges from love and concern is reshaped by the delivery or severity of message, driving a wedge where none is needed.

Outlook, lifestyle, behavior and action that is harmful

The probability of working in close proximity to deviancy for twenty-five years and emerging without a telltale scar or behavior issue is slim to non-existent. Encounters that range the gamut of inhumanity and violence, needless death and destruction and a host of other negative events take a toll on the human psyche. It leaves a residue of emotional and physiological damage.

Consider this statement:

> "*A career spent immersed in society's problems,*
> *investigating violence, providing care and custody to people*
> *who victimize other humans, responding to dangerous and*
> *intense situations and being an observer of the worst in*
> *society, corrodes the individual's sense of right from wrong,*

---

[4] . Goldbaum, E. (2012). Police officer stress creates significant health risks compared to a general population. http://www.buffalo.edu/news/releases/2012/07/13532.html

safety and well-being. The journey takes its toll, one day at a time. As the years pass the once robust and healthy person is burdened with numerous negative physical and mental health issues that erode his or her life and those of family, friends, and peers far quicker than other careers" Lumb et al (2009)[5].

This leaves little doubt about the intense trauma that can and does occur. Damage to oneself, family, peers and others in the social environment is often irreversible and whose outcome is further diminishment of one's soul.

<u>The effect of stress on physical, psychological, and emotional systems.</u>

Issues that accompany stress and adversity are numerous and harmful to the individual's emotional and physical health. Routine work stressors are a constant presence in the life of police and first responders, higher than most other occupations (Biggs, Brough, Barbour, 2014)[6]. The greater propensity of exposure to violence, danger, life and death decisions, accompanying influence of legal, organizational, ethical, and social forces tend to weigh heavily on officers. These factors thrive as vulnerable occupational groups attempt to bring order to chaos, make sense of the nonsensical, and meet the expectations of so many others whose view of what they do is external or distant from the actual practices.

We know that the effects of accumulated stress and adversity are damaging and contribute to dysfunction and the early death of many. We often see first responders with respiratory, heart and weight problems. The existence of back trouble, higher mortality for cancer, and abusive substance use is all too common. The extended damage to family and social relationships exceeds that of the general public. Divorce and suicide rates of police and other first responder occupational groups are higher than that of the general public. Williams and Huber (1986:246[7]) discussed symptoms of stress providing the following comprehensive list:

"This occupational group harbors higher than normal negative emotions and attitudes and they often see the world in either black or white terms and anyone who is not close to them is generally considered an "asshole", a common descriptor of someone not in close proximity to their philosophy or beliefs. As the years on the job roll onward, so too does the list of people who are not trusted and who are suspect and demand close watching. This often includes administrators, Judges, and anyone who disagrees or is not supportive. We also find a shift in humor from funny jokes to sick humor where degradation and accusatory or demeaning stories are told and often

[5] Lumb, R., Breazeale, R., Lumb, P., & Metz, G. (2009). Public Safety Officer Emotional Health: Addressing the Silent Killer. The Correctional Trainer. Fall.

[6] Biggs, A., Brough, P., and Barbour, J. (2014). Exposure to extra-organization stressor: Impact on mental health and organization perceptions for police officers. International Journal of Stress Management © 2014 American Psychological Association. 2014, Vol. 21, No. 3, 255-282

[7] Williams, J. C., and Huber, G. P. 1986. *Human Behavior in Organizations*. Cincinnati, OH: South-Western Publishing.

focused on the down trodden individuals that they often encounter. Gallows humor also seems to become more prominent in these vulnerable occupations."

Over time the trust factor dwindles and strangers, even those wearing the same uniform, will not be initially trusted. It takes time to work your way in and even less time to lose the trust of others, if you stray from the intended agenda. Officers will quickly take sides when another of their ranks is accused regardless of evidence to the contrary. The closing of ranks and circling the wagons is not altogether healthy. Whether the threat is actual or anticipated, defensive action occurs before any deed takes place.

Time diminishes engagement in outside of job activities and for some; they are only interested in job related events. Their identity is the badge, uniform or to associate oneself as a member of a special organization. Sometimes, this can take on paranoid dimensions. Being prepared, carrying the tools of one's trade, identifying with the profession, and some level of caution and suspicion, recognized by the constant scanning of one's environment, are all indicators of personality and attitude. The impact on family, peers, friends and others can be discerned as there is a gradual pulling away and distancing from these other groups. When feelings associated with the job are conflicted, these thoughts often result in expressions of concern or down right complaint.

Often, negative views and outlooks will result in the following outcomes:

- Diminished job performance
- Disruptive behavior
- Behavior that may result in liability to the organization
- Increased subjectivity to discipline
- Impaired judgment
- Health issues
- Alienation from others
- Burnout
- Job loss (resignation or dismissal)
- Morale issue on peers
- Erosion of public confidence

Symptoms of Stress

Selye (1946)[8] described the phases that the body goes through in response to a threat. Referred to as "The *general adaptation syndrome"* model. The body encounters three stages that are:

1. Alarm reaction. As one's body prepares for an emergency, several physiological changes take place. They include:

---

[8] Selye, H. 1946. "The general adaptation syndrome and the diseases of adaptation." *Journal of Clinical Endocrinology*. 2: 117-230.

- Digestion slows down,
- Heart beats faster,
- Dilation of the blood vessels dilate,
- Increase in blood pressure,
- Breathing is rapid and deep,
- Bodily systems collaborate to provide maximum energy for fight or flight.

2. <u>Resistance</u>. As exposure to stress continues or increases our system will seek to compensate and increase tolerance. If stress is ongoing and continues, the body will use energy to strengthen and help shield the person from future stress. It will also wear down one's system over time. We are not invincible.

3. <u>Exhaustion</u>. At that point when energy is all used up or depleted, the alarm reactions return, and stress manifests itself as an illness often as heart ailment, ulcers, or high blood pressure, as three examples.

Selye (p. 10) illustrated at that time how during early days of civilization, encounters with danger triggered the fight or flight response as it was often necessary for survival. Today's nervous system still responds in the same manner, but the environment is not the same, reducing response requirement. So, has the body compensated and is no longer affected by stressful situations? No, not in the least! Reitz (1987)[9]

Reitz (1987:239) writes that individuals in modern society often substitute other psychological reactions for flight-or-flight situations. They include negativism, expression of boredom, dissatisfaction, irritability, anger over unimportant matters, and feelings of persecution. Substitutions for fleeing include apathy, resignation, fantasy, forgetfulness, inability to concentrate, procrastination, and inability to make decisions.

Short-term stress has served a useful purpose in our survival. Long-term stress, however, involves increasingly higher levels of prolonged and uninterrupted stress. The body adapts to the stress by gradually adjusting its baseline to higher and higher levels. For example, workers in stressful jobs often show an increased "resting" heart rate. Pelletier (1977) believes that the deleterious effects of stress are created only by unrelieved long-term stress.

Albrecht[10] (1979:119) believes that the effects of stress are cumulative in nature. Ulcers do not just happen overnight in a high stress situation; they are generally the result of long extended exposure to stress. "The health breakdown is simply the logical conclusion of a self-induced disease development over a period of 10 to 20 years."

---

[9] Reitz, H. J. 1986. *Behavior in Organizations*. Homewood, IL: Irwin.
[10] Albrecht, K. 1979. *Stress and the Manager*. Englewood Cliffs, NJ: Prentice-Hall.

Williams and Huber[11] (1986:264) provide an expanded list of the symptoms of stress that may have a negative effect on physical and emotional health. Their list includes the following:

- Constant fatigue
- Low energy level
- Recurring headaches
- Gastrointestinal disorders
- Chronically bad breath
- Sweaty hands or feet
- Dizziness
- High blood pressure
- Pounding heart
- Constant inner tension
- Inability to sleep
- Temper outbursts
- Hyperventilation
- Moodiness
- Irritability and restlessness
- Inability to concentrate
- Increased aggression
- Compulsive eating
- chronic worrying
- Anxiety or apprehensiveness
- Inability to relax
- Growing feelings of inadequacy
- Increase in defensiveness
- Dependence on tranquilizers
- Excessive use of alcohol
- Excessive smoking

Personal performance is affected by stress. Half of all workers say that job stress reduces their productivity (Lawless, 1992). McGrath[12] (1976) reports that mild to moderate amounts of stress allow people to perform more effectively. It should not continue forever as eventually it will harm the individual and decrease performance and will be harmful to the individual health. McGrath reports that stress leads to emotional and physiological symptoms and brings about changes in the individual's attitude. This may include paranoia, undue caution, increased suspicion and hostility with skewed reality observations. In policing, this is a serious outcome and one that we need not allow to happen.

In policing, public safety and first responder jobs, the individual often experiences one or more of the following situations:

1) Negative encounters;

---

[11] Williams, J. C., and Huber, G. P. 1986. *Human Behavior in Organizations*. Cincinnati, OH: South-Western Publishing.

[12] McGrath, J. E. 1976. "Stress and behavior in organizations." In *Handbook of Industrial and Organizational Psychology*. Dunnett, M. D. (Ed) Chicago: Rand McNally College Publishing.

2) Seeing, smelling, tasting encounters with danger and deviance;
3) Devil may care attitude by members of the public;
4) The attitude that we keep trying and nothing changes;
5) Administration is out of touch and does not care;
6) Role conflicts resulting from overload, lack of training, unreasonable expectations;
7) The never changing environment, loss of belief and hope.

Unfortunately, the effects of stress and trauma eventually transfers to the family. Peers and friends are also drawn into the fray and as the pressure builds the framework of personal balance is shattered and begins to disintegrate. One negative outcome that is mentioned repeatedly in this manuscript is the high divorce rate of this occupational group.

Personal Symptoms and Impact.

A. Physical manifestations or health issues include a thickening of the heart's left ventricle, or chamber, a condition that often precedes coronary heart disease and heart attacks (Pieper, 1990[13]).

B. Psychological abrasions that generally do not improve without help.

C. Emotional trauma and short circuited ability to act and be normal.

D. Transfer the dysfunction to others including family, friends, and peers.

When we are aware that help is needed we must take steps. Waiting for positive change to occur may not happen as desired. The job environment is such that continuation of the conditions that produce stress do not abate and the levels of stress remain high. Symptoms of uncaring, anger, criticism of the agency, administrators and others persists, frustration and despair and other negativity is unhealthy for the individual and those with whom he or she works, their family and friends, and others with whom they share life.

Address short and long-term individual, occupational and community adversity

The focus of resilience training is prevention oriented. It provides individuals' and groups with training in durability, building skills and knowledge that help people to respond appropriately, to manage emotional reaction, strengthen well-being, reduce damaging stress related outcomes, and seek a more harmonious and balanced lifestyle.

When a substantial incident or event occurs, people react utilizing a complex array of physical, emotional, mental and behavior responses. Whatever the traumatic event, economic crisis, life threatening event, loss of job, confronting extreme danger, natural or manmade disaster for example, the results generate common responses and behaviors (Jaukovi', 2002). The first reaction is shock, then fear and a desire or belief that rescue help is on the way or can be found. Steps are generally taken to engage in rational acts and seeking a restoration to normalcy and balance. People experience

---

[13] Pieper, C. 1990. "Job stress can physically change your heart, study finds." In the *Minneapolis Star/Tribune*. April 11.

euphoria for surviving and that is soon followed by the sobering realization of what happened and what exists. Unless help is obvious and hope is forthcoming, many experience depression and a wide range of moods at the reality they are experiencing. In time, people begin to reorganize and develop strategies and pathways that lead to new outcomes. Reactions by individuals and groups include reflex to the situation, a continued functionality, and control of cognitive and social behaviors.

Understanding Adversity

Encountering hardship, danger, harsh conditions, trauma and other situations that are challenging and carry some risk to health and welfare can be deemed adversarial. Adversity in its many forms may elicit a reaction that can range from being startled to feelings of being overwhelmed. The effects of a prior traumatic event may attach itself to a current incident of adversity exacerbating the emotional response. Negativity may manifest itself along a continuum of mere acknowledgement through resistance or in some instances withdrawal. Willingness to take steps to overcome the challenge requires inner fortitude and drawing on one's inner durability skills. For some who work in an environment that presents danger and negativity on a regular basis, coming to terms with the need to maintain a positive attitude and outlook may be difficult.

Some may suffer from life-long symptoms and oftentimes accept a condition as a natural outcome of life. Perhaps the manifestation emerges from an external influence resulting in a desire to bring about positive change. People react to negative emotional stimuli in the following ways:

- Tolerance and forgiving nature.
- React negatively and seek revenge.
- Shy away, feel bothered for some time after the event.
- Adopt a 'why me" attitude, engage in self-blame.
- Anticipate self-blame from others.
- Experience loss of hope for something better.

The effects of long-term adversity and stress may result in physical and emotional health issues. These will impact your ability to perform duties, maintain stamina, and keep a clear and positive attitude without falling victim to long-term negativity. Other manifestations of long-term stress include the potential loss of family, friends, peers, and one's job. Adversity and stress impact on relationships. Breaking free of the stressors is difficult and requires understanding and a willingness to begin the change process. Adversarial outcomes negatively affect a person's well-being in the following ways:

> **Mental**:   Anxiety, flawed decision-making, poor disposition, restlessness, feeling overwhelmed and burnout.

> **Physical**:   Respiratory, heart, weight changes, back trouble, higher mortality, cancer, loss energy, tension in neck, sleep problems.

28

> **Social**:   High divorce, diminishing circle of friends, distrust of others, and alienation.

Illustration.

Carl had worked at the Maine State Prison for twenty-seven years. Three more years to his retirement. Returning home from his shift one day he was informed by his wife that she was leaving him. He did not see it coming and was completely taken back by the news.

Resorting to drinking alcohol when off duty, he stopped associating with his friend that he frequently went fishing with, did not eat properly and often called out on sick leave, something he had not done in his 27 years with the department. When at work he was sullen and quiet, seemed lethargic, and while present was not doing the job in a safe manner. His supervisor knew about the pending divorce and figured that time would be best cure. The supervisor asked others on the shift to step up until the issue became better and they agreed.

Carl did not show up for work one shift and they figured he needed a day off and had forgotten to call. The second day he did not appear the Prison called the County Sheriff to check. The Deputy that went to Carl's house found him dead, an apparent suicide.

Related Inquiry Questions

Q.1: What was the responsibility of the supervisor?

Q.2: What was the responsibility of Carl's peers, if any?

Q.3: What should the policy state to address employee work related issues?

Q.4: What might the role of the department be to address working in a high stress environment for years?

Q.5: Other comments?

Jaukovi'[14] (2002) provides responses to a person's internal demand for survival during a crisis stage as including the following eight strategies:

1. Need to rescue others

2. Attachment to a rescuer

3. Asserting and achieving goals

4. Adapting and surrendering to the situation

5. Fighting to remove danger and adversity

---

[14] Jaukovi', Jelena. (2002) The Manners of Overcoming Stress Generated by War Conflict Trauma. European Journal of Crime, Criminal Law and Criminal Justice, Vol. 10/2-3, 177-181.

6. Fleeing to get away from danger;

7. Competing for scarce essentials;

8. Cooperating to create essentials for the groups' survival.

Maladaptive responses contribute to increased trauma and strain that can exacerbate feelings of hopelessness and anxiety. Reactions of manifested behaviors observed when someone is highly anxious and distraught include fear, despair, rage, anger, and withdrawal, the inability to react or function normally, and sleep disorder. Other responses include anti-social behavior, aggression, feelings of revenge, substance abuse, abandonment, criminality, and alienation. When a person experiences severe trauma or adversity, he or she will draw upon their knowledge, skills and experience to address the situation and overcome the problems. Endurance training provides pre-event and preventive options that can assist and strengthen a person prior to an event, thereby reducing the overall trauma and recovery period.

Identifying and addressing warning signs of stress and adversity

Government, public/private organizations, communities and individuals experience hardship, danger, and misfortune to varying degrees as a normal component of conducting business. Events occur that span a continuum from stressful to disastrous. They create situations where recovery to a sense of normalcy and well-being is difficult. Experiencing similar situations, we accumulate psychological, physiological and social manifestations that are unhealthy and potentially damaging to the individual.

When conditions cause stress and disrupt our ability to manage them we may experience emotional, health, work related or relationship problems resulting in further dysfunction. Sadly, examples are numerous. We often see individuals, who have reached their threshold of tolerance, react with defensive behaviors displaying anger, withdrawal, increased use of alcohol, disrupted sleep, display impatience toward others, and a host of other previously stated manifestations that we label as unusual or unwarranted. After-the-fact official response generally takes the form of discipline, dismissal, or abandonment, and ostracized by others. In some instances this leads to extreme health problems, disability and occasionally death. Regardless of outcomes, unless the problem is addressed, the individual will continue to spiral downward into a deepening depression and a more difficult recovery.

Accumulated stress, negative life events and frequent adversarial encounters

A) Emotional Manifestations.

1. Anxiety. Feel uptight, nervous, anticipation of negativity, fear the future. Tend to worry about things that may not require attention and concern but due to anxiety have difficulty in setting them aside.

2. Anger. Negative reaction to those things you disagree with. Find certain behavior irritating and you condemn and complain about them. Short fuse and blow off at others.

3. Irritable. Small issues bother you and cause frustration or anxiety. Issues you cannot change are troubling and you dwell on them (i.e., the economy).

4. Depression / Feel overwhelmed / Other issues. People with depressive illnesses do not experience all the same symptoms. The severity, frequency and duration of symptoms will vary depending on the individual and his or other particular illness.

Symptoms include:

A. Persistent sad, anxious or "empty" feelings.
B. Feelings of hopelessness and/or pessimism.
C. Feelings of guilt, worthlessness and/or helplessness.
D. Irritability, restlessness.
E. Loss of interest in activities or hobbies once pleasurable, including sex.
F. Fatigue and decreased energy.
G. Difficulty concentrating, remembering details and making decisions.
H. Insomnia, early-morning wakefulness, or excessive sleeping
I   Overeating or appetite loss.
J. Thoughts of suicide, suicide attempts.
K. Persistent aches or pains, headaches, cramps or digestive problems that do not ease even with treatment.

5. Poor disposition. Not able to find satisfaction or happiness in your situation or those things you experience. Normally take the negative and anticipate things to get worse. Feel that the world is going to hell in a hand basket. And often see people in a negative way.

ILLUSTRATION

Ellen had been married to Frank for eight years. There were no children and both she and her husband worked full-time jobs. They owned their own home, had new cars, a boat and the latest electronic equipment.

As was Frank's habit he would go out for "a beer" with the boys after work and would not get home until after the normal supper hour. Ellen eventually stopped preparing meals and would eat alone. There was no negative attitude or problem with Frank, but it was not setting well with Ellen and she, on more than one occasion, said something about her perceptions. Ellen's anger was resulting in a short temper both at home and at work and her long-term view of the future was cloudy.

Related Inquiry Questions

Q.1: If you were asked to intervene, what would your plan be and what are the key points you would address?

Q.2: Are there follow-up needs and, if so, what might they be?

B) Physiological Manifestations.

Not only emotional triggers appear due to stress, we also suffer from physical discomfort, as the following story illustrates

---

John was a Psychologist in a state mental health clinic. With the economy and unemployment in the tank, his agency was swamped and it required John's working evenings and occasionally on a Saturday.

His wife and children were complaining about his not being home much and that the normal house responsibilities were falling behind, all of which added to the stress.

John noticed that on occasion his heart seemed to "flutter" and that he sometimes seemed out of breath. Not getting proper sleep also had him feeling tired and fidgety.

Coming home late last evening he and his wife got into an argument about his long hours and not being home.

Related Inquiry Questions

Q.1: What must happen?

Q.2: If you were John's supervisor, what would you do?

Q.3: Other comments.

C) Social relationships including family, friends and peers.

Individuals experiencing emotional, psychological and physiological issues often increases pressure on family and loved ones, colleagues and others with whom they associate. Common are the following negative outcomes.

1. Widening distance between people
2. Diminished communication and engagement with others
3. Nitpicking and complaining
4. Exercise greater control
5. Find fault needlessly
6. Cautious and protective stance in life
7. Arguments over trivial matters
8. Unhappiness with current conditions
9. Psychological impact on children
10. Separation and divorce
11. Violence and legal issues

ILLUSTRATION

Jobs that demand multiple people working in harmony, especially in times of great stress, require that members of the team mesh well and collaborate in a seamless manner. Many occupations come to mind and include Coast Guard, Police, Fire, Emergency Management, Emergency Room medical, combat units, deck crew on an aircraft carrier and dozens of others.

If one member of the group is experiencing severe stress due to family, work, health, financial or other contributing element, it can and will affect the harmony of the group due to distraction, stress, and worry about fixing the personal problem. People have withdrawn from normal social relationships, taken more sick leave than normal, been short tempered, and other outward manifestations while continuing to work.

Sara had been a member of the problem-solving unit for three years. Each member of the group brought specific skills and knowledge to their work responsibilities and it generally resulted in sustainable outcomes. With an increase of work demands, many hours of overtime were required. This had a negative impact on Sara as her family was experiencing her absence and it was also showing in their behavior.

Attempting to compensate, Sara was taking available sick leave, allowing her to remain at home more and provide her family needed attention. Her absence at work resulted in late project completion, she was less willing to take on additional work, and often was critical when not called for. When questioned, she was argumentative and defensive toward here colleagues. This was having a negative impact on the people she worked with increasing their overall level of stress.

Related Inquiry Questions

Q.1: What are the larger implications of this scenario?

Q.2: What should be done about the problem as described?

Q.3: What would you do if the supervisor of the group?

Q.4: Other comments.

D) Employment and Civil Responsibilities.

Employers hire and expect a level of performance that retains service mandates, is cost effective and efficient, keeps problems to a minimum, and offers employee focus on mission and goals of the organization. Stress, adversity and trauma throw these expectations asunder, diminishing all expectations and resulting in dysfunction and disruption. Common manifestations of disruption include:

1. Diminished job performance

2. Lowered productivity
3. Disruptive behavior
4. Liability concerns
5. Impaired judgment
6. Increased subjectivity to discipline
7. Argumentative exchanges
8. Excessive complaints from staff
9. Registering of high number of complaints from clients
10. Division among employees
11. Increased grievances
12. Avoid engagement
13. Overreaction
14. Higher than normal disciplinary conferences

ILLUSTRATION

A police officer had been disciplined twice for over-reacting when dealing with members of a Latino community. He argued that the youth he was talking with were disrespectful and it required "getting their attention" which included swearing and talking in a loud voice. His Sergeant told the officer to *"knock it off or face discipline."*

Complaining with his peers, the officer said he was going to turn a blind eye to all problems in that neighborhood from now on. They could go screw themselves for all he cared.

Related Inquiry Questions

Q.1: What is wrong with this scenario?

Q.2: What is a better way to handle the situation as a supervisor?

Q.3: What are some of the outcomes of not doing anything further?

Q.4: Other thoughts?

More often than not, response to dysfunction and manifestations of improper behavior are post-event actions designed to "fix" the problem. They usually include behavior change mandates, threat or actual discipline, supervisor intervention, duty or work transfer and other actions that may not be completely successful. If the employee fails to appropriately respond a hardening of supervisor attitude occurs and additional distance exacerbates the situation. Then the actions by all parties become more extreme and generally not successful in recovery. This scenario is all too common and represents a failure of the post-event approach. Changing behavior and restoring a person to a balanced lifestyle does not begin after the problem has manifested itself, it must begin early in the process when subtle signs and symptoms are observed.

An identified need exists to help individuals, groups, organizations and communities adopt a prevention based model of overall health building. The goal is to develop appropriate durability skills that minimize trauma associated with exposure to adverse conditions. The cost of prevention or mitigation of traumatic events is substantially less than responding to a post-event crisis. Long-term negative outcomes can be minimized by addressing issues before they manifest into a crisis to substantially reduce the overall harmful outcomes. Illustrations from recent history are replete with examples of elevated trauma because individuals, groups and communities were not prepared for the terrible outcomes they experienced.

A personal example involves my involvement in a traffic accident. On duty as a State Police Officer and experiencing the death of another person and injury to me, brings forth many questions about the causes and contributing factors. What might have been done to avoid the collision? Following hospitalization and recovery I returned to light duty while physical healing continued. No one that I worked with, or within the department, made further mention of the accident. The State Police did not inquire further nor did they require my consulting with anyone. The accident was deemed the other operator's fault, seemingly sufficient for all parties. While I like to think my recovery went well, there are times I think about the incident and the person who was killed. Recovery is long and the lingering traumatic effects remain in place for years. As someone once told me, "*You don't get over it, you get through it.*"

In contrast, to those situations where signals of dysfunction and other examples of problems arise, waiting until something happens to act is itself imprudent. Programs focused on prevention increase awareness, instill confidence, and provide opportunity to plan for and address problems, adversity, crisis and trauma before they occur and become untenable.

<u>Purpose of Book Summary</u>

The purpose of this book is to identify and describe the effects of accumulated stress, adversity and trauma on your life and its effect on the life of family, friends, co-workers and peers. Training provides strategies to overcome and combat debilitating events accelerating a return to a more balanced, productive and comfortable lifestyle. When an individual experiences overwhelming pressure, the cause of which might be job related, a health issue, external event, or gradual accumulation of negative events, to name a few countless causes, eventually change will occur. This change may be in behavior and attitude, splintered emotions, physical health issues, job performance concerns, and social relationship transformation, all of which are often negative in nature.

For an organization there are cost issues, concern for disrupted work performance, tension with other workers and supervisors and important considerations of safety and well-being. Service delivery may be affected and customer or client satisfaction will be impacted negatively. Adversity often leads to confrontation. The traumatizing results generally impact on others who witness or are participants in the same unit or function. When an employee experiences anxiety, strain, or burden there are generally observable signs or symptoms; if, someone is paying attention. Unfortunately, many peers, supervisors and others ignore them and prefer to wait it out rationalizing that "ole Tom will work out of it in due time and it is none of our business." This is wrong thinking, especially when problems exacerbate and take a negative path, diminishing normal process and finding a sustainable solution to problem solving.

Within organizations, people generally belong to or work within a group performing similar duties or product development. Groups are affected by the dysfunction of one or more individuals and unless addressed it is disruptive and divisive increasing tension, animosity, and open confrontation. Individuals within groups may choose sides, be protective or accusatory, and all manner of behavior may be observed while the dysfunction is present. Even passive or harmless causes of imbalance create an atmosphere that inhibits effectiveness and efficiency due to distraction and attention to the offending problem.

In a world that seems selfish, divisive, and in some cases with a "*To hell with others*" attitude, we must find ways to reach middle ground that does not compromise service and mission accomplishment. It is not about the individual in an organizational perspective, it is about people doing the job expected, acclimating to duty and being able to manage self-attitude and action.

Communities are also affected by events and situations that disrupt the normal lifestyles and normality that precedes the triggering event. Awareness of an issue leads to gossip, demands for intervention, pressure on elected and appointed officials to take action, and other disruptive intercessions aimed at restoring harmony. When the disruption affects the whole community, the need for collaborative and unified action is dependent on planning, preparation, training, available resources, and other elements that lead to successful outcomes. A disaster or traumatic event is numbing and disrupts the normal aspects of the community. This makes it difficult, to near impossible, to react in a simultaneous and forthright manner. These same conditions exist within individuals, groups and organizations and they are debilitating and disruptive to normal operations.

Thus, we are directed to the need for a collaborative prevention model, one that anticipates and provides the requisite skills. This model would provide knowledge to allow individuals, groups, communities and others to address issues or catastrophic events with minimal distraction resulting in adequate responses. The Durability model identifies indicators of stress, adversity, trauma and other debilitating identifiers and provides strategies to assist someone or group return to a more balanced lifestyle or harmonious work environment.

Chapter 3
Organization Contributors

Agency Responsibility

When we hire someone for a job that carries high stress, the potential of danger and personal harm, where traumatic events occur and we send our employees to handle them, we owe them more than wages and benefits. Unlike other less physical and psychologically damaging jobs, police and first responders engage in daily situations of elevated risk and within an environment that most people avoid.

A. <u>What are the priorities?</u>

<u>Fact</u>: organizations are responsible for their employee's s well-being and health. This applies not only to dangers associated with the job but must also address emotional and psychological well-being. When an employee displays unusual behavior that is out of character with prior performance, supervisor attention is warranted. Issues range from excessive sick leave, a reduction in performance, argumentative with co-workers or supervisor, being late for work, displaying unusual mood shifts, negative comments, and displays of frustration or potential angry outbursts. These represent stress and adversity issues and require supervisory attention.

Organizations establish rules and then consider their job done. They expect employees to follow these rules and for supervisors to enforce employee compliance. If that were the case, existing issues would be non-detectable. However, it is unrealistic to believe that the existence of rules and policy is sufficient. Rules are guidelines to behavior and performance. They are important and critical to the organization in maintaining its responsibility to its legal issues, mission, operational, maintenance of its existence and its core services and products. However, rules are not capable of human awareness, for they are only concerned with employee performance and compliance.

B. <u>Equipment for the body.</u>

Technology has elevated body protection devices to minimize injury and potential death resulting from traumatic and forceful attack. One example is the latest lightweight, flexible body armor that is 15 times stronger than steel. Remarkably, it weighs only 10 pounds when constructed into a layered suit. The armor will protect against Level I threats and protect police officers from low velocity .40 and 9 mm ammunition. With an average of 60 police officers killed by gunshot each year, body protection is critical.

Officers are provided with weapons, reinforced vehicles, and other protection devices to keep injury at a minimum, avoid contact with bodily fluid and non-lethal weapons to use when minimum force is required other than physical engagement. The point being, we have a done an outstanding job protecting officers from injury, contamination, and exposure to harmful elements that our police and first responder personnel might encounter. As our military develops new strategies, devices, and protective equipment, it is transferrable to our civilian police, fire, corrections, EMT, and other public safety officers. Research, manufacturer and sales of protective equipment are active in the police and first responder's field. Far less discussed and locking in focus is in the protection of emotional, psychological well-being and the resulting manifestations to the effects of stress, adversity and trauma and their impact to the individual's health.

C. Addressing the psychological and emotional issues.

Police and first responders frequently come face to face with all manner of inhumanity, trauma, dangerous situations, and violence in the course of normal duty. It can be conceded that daily encounters with violence and its aftermath are not uncommon. However, being in a constant state of vigilance, results in high levels of anticipation that may elevate body response functions above the norm. Over time, these encounters accumulate and lodge within the individual causing an elevated anticipation and wariness of events and people that cause a rise of stress levels.

Albrecht (1979)[15] provides four categories of emotionally induced stress that are created within the individual. They are:

1) Time stress created by real or imaginary deadlines,
2) Anticipatory when the perceived event is seen as unpleasant.
3) Situational when a person worries about outcomes of an event.
4) Encounter stress with both pleasant and unpleasant people.

All manner of environmental events may trigger stress. These include work demands or conversely too little work productivity, lack of job security and environmental conditions of smell, noise, and other environmental conditions. The individual becomes unsure of role and expectations may experience conflict with peers or supervisors, and experience a lack of input leading to feelings of isolation (Reitz, 1987)[16].

When we consider patrol time, those hours spent in the cruiser and answering calls or in personal interest activities (i.e., traffic enforcement), we know much of that time is less stressful than anticipated (Brooks & Piquero, 1998[17]; Piquero, 2005[18]; Swatt, Gibson, & Piquero, 2007[19]). What we term routine, such as answering calls from

---

[15] http://www.mindtools.com/pages/article/albrecht-stress.htm

[16] Reitz, H. J. 1986. *Behavior in Organizations*. Homewood, IL: Irwin.

[17] Brooks, L., & Piquero, N. (1998). Police stress: Does department size matter? *Policing, 21,*

600-617.

[18] Piquero, N. (2005). Understanding police stress and coping resources across gender: A look towards general strain theory. In H. Copes (Ed.), *Policing and stress* (pp. 126-139). Upper Saddle River, NJ: Prentice Hall.

[19] Swatt, M., Gibson, C., & Piquero, N. (2007). Exploring the utility of general strain theory in explaining problematic alcohol consumption by police officers. *Journal of Criminal Justice,*

citizens, who may have limited information and who report something unusual happening at a place known for danger and threat to the officer, expectations rise about potential for harm. The body reacts in anticipation and chronic stress can accrue and have a significant impact on the individual over time (Crank, 1998[20]; Regehr, LeBlanc, Jelley, & Barath, 2008[21]). Results range from hyperactivity, psychological and physical health problems, alcohol and drug abuse, burnout, and relationship problems with family, friends and peers.

Volumes have been written about the effects of adversity and stress on police and first responders who encounter all manner of deviance in their daily work. Concern for their stress has been a vexing issue for decades. The question is not if the effects of trauma will cause negative outcomes, but when? The question before us is: How do we protect personnel from harmful outcomes?

D. Policy: Include emotional and psychological health needs.

Luck is useful when purchasing a lottery ticket. However, employee health, the foundation of productive human resources, should not be left to chance. The issues and problems are far too common. No responsible executive will or should ignore the many issues common with long-term exposure to stress, adversity and trauma. Employee health should be a clear wellness policy that delineates what and how the organization will seek to protect the individual from harmful outcomes.

The Derbyshire Constabulary in England has a policy addressing the psychological well-being of their employees[22]. Their policy statement is:

> *The organization is committed to facilitating and promoting psychological well-being of staff and to developing strategies to actively address stress related issues. It is intended that this policy will complement existing initiatives to promote behaviors that will not tolerate unacceptable behavior within the workplace, which may contribute to stress.*
>
> *Guidance will be provided to staff within the organization with regard to measures aimed at addressing workplace stress and a comprehensive approach will be developed to promoting psychological well-being. The policy will support the development of a year on year program of addressing reducing stress and promoting psychological well-being in the organization. These will ensure early intervention as well as promoting preventative measures as being a much better strategy to managing this issue.*

To insure that a constant and consistent level of attention and assistance is provided, the organization should implement a policy with relevant procedures. A

35, 596-611.

[20] Crank, J. (1998). *Understanding police culture*. Cincinnati, OH: Anderson.

[21] Regehr, C., LeBlanc, V., Jelley, R. B., & Barath, I. (2008). Acute stress and performance in police recruits. *Stress and Health, 24,* 295-303.

[22]

https://www.google.com/#q=Derbyshire+Constabulary+in+England+has+a+policy+addressing+the+psychological+well+being+

policy outlines the values, intent, actions, and support that will be provided, when needed and without stigma or personal injury.

E. <u>Programs that address cause, symptoms, and strategies to maintain balance in life.</u>

Albrecht[23] (1979) theorized that there were eight universal factors that come into play when job satisfaction is achieved, thereby reducing stress and adversity. Employees will vary in their individual level of comfort at work and management can improve balance and reduce stress when they implement programs and policy to address the following:

1. Job status.
2. Accountability standards.
3. Extent of human contact.
4. Extent of physical challenge.
5. Mental/emotional challenge.
6. Variety of job tasks undertaken.
7. Workload on the individual employee.
8. Physical conditions and environment of the individual's work.

<u>SKAME Model[24]</u>

Each employee has individual strengths and abilities and will perform their duties based on their individual skills, knowledge, abilities, motivation and experience (Albrecht; 1979; Williams and Huber, 1986[25]). They offered action steps that managers can implement to reduce stress in the workplace. They are:

1. Clear and unambiguous work assignments, limits of responsibility and authority, and how employee performance will be evaluated.
2. Introduce the manager's leadership style and secure employee understanding.
3. Delegate effectively and empower subordinates where it is situationally feasible.
4. Be clear in establishing and conveying goals and decision–making criteria.
5. Establish work and vacation policies for all employees.

Lawless (1991)[26] identified employer programs effective in helping employees with stress, adversity and burn out. He stated the results were reduced levels of employee burn out and a lowered stress related illness, at a reduced cost. The programs are:

1. Flexible work hours.
2. Supportive work and family policy.

---

[23] Albrecht, K. 1979. *Stress and the Manager.* Englewood Cliffs, NJ: Prentice-Hall.

[24] The role of management is to determine job fit with the individual's SKAM Albrecht, K. 1979. *Stress and the Manager.* Englewood Cliffs, NJ: Prentice-Hall.

[25] Williams, J. C., and Huber, G. P. 1986. *Human Behavior in Organizations.* Cincinnati, OH: South-Western Publishing. Not treat all employees as a *"one size fits all"* to elicit maximum performance with minimum stress and adversity.

[26] Lawless, P. 1992. *Empllis,* MN: Northwestern National Life Employee Benefits Division.

3. Effective communications by management with employees
4. Health insurance that covers mental health and chemical dependency issues.
5. Steps to increase personal durability and lower negative effects of stress, adversity, trauma or disaster.

As people, we handle adversity using a variety of strategies that we have acquired and which are shaped by culture, society, family and others.

<u>Factors that constitute Endurance</u>.

1. Awareness of your feelings.
2. Optimism and outlook on life.
3. Ability to confront and deal with feelings.

We will discuss these in more detail when we consider strategies to reduce adversity and stress and increase our personal Durability.

Figure 1.1

The Resiliency Wheel[27]
Steps organizations and groups can take to restore balance

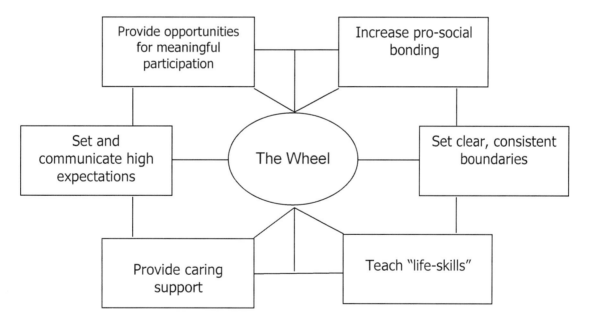

[27]. The Resiliency Training Program, 1977, Nan Henderson & Associates

Explaining the Wheel

Left Side of Wheel	Right Side of the Wheel
Provide Opportunities for meaningful Participation: Help individuals determine ways they can address the crisis themselves. Working through problems and finding solutions is therapeutic and can lead a person to restored life balance. **Set and Communicate High Expectations:** Express your certainty that individuals can cope with the situation and that they will be able to draw on their strength and inner resources to recover and move ahead. **Provide Caring and Support:** Listen to individual concerns and answer their questions in a direct, factual, and honest way. Truth, while sometimes painful, is the only way to help people confront demons and move forward.	**Increase Pro-Social Bonding:** Help people find positive activities that address the issues and provide a sense of purpose that leads to mastery of the situation. **Set Clear and Consistent Boundaries:** Help people find a balance between addressing concerns and getting back to a normal schedule. The safety of familiar rules and routines cannot be overlooked. **Teach Life skills:** Encourage individuals to communicate their thoughts and feelings. Discussion should not dwell on the negative and should always address positive ideas, seek solutions to identified problems, and offer a balanced, not overwhelming process forward.

For more information on crisis response and counseling, check out these websites.

- SAMSHA: http://www.samhsa.gov/ (click on crisis counseling)
- U.S. Department of Education: http://www.ed.gov
- UCLA: smhp.psych.ucla.edu (select topics of Crisis Prevention and Response, Grief and Bereavement, or Post-Traumatic Stress.

Durability training: Community, organizational and people

Each of us has a story that illustrates how durability played an important role at some point in our life. Events occur and we are seldom prepared to respond in a planned manner. It might be a traffic accident, fire, health issue, or other trauma inducing circumstance. When an event occurs we must be able to draw upon knowledge and skills that allow resistance and recovery.

Acquiring durability skills and knowledge provides the following strengths and strategies useful to formulating an appropriate response.

1. Remain flexible in your thoughts and actions when addressing a difficult situation.

2. Dig deep within personal strengths eliciting stamina to overcome a problem.

3. Remain strong and tough to get through the problem encountered.

4. Be durable and quick to recover rather than wallow in grief and indecision.

5. Adjust to the difficult situation and come out ahead.

During times of extreme stress and adversity it is important to be able to persist and continue to move forward when doing something different or seeking to avoid engagement would be easier. This is very difficult. The confusion and disbelief that accompanies any traumatic or adverse event can become the dominant control agent of one's thinking.

There are occupations where continuous confrontation with stressful and often dangerous situations exists that will immerse the individual in an endless loop of pressure depending on circumstance and situation. Common stressful occupations include correctional officers, fire, EMT, police, mental health provider, emergency room doctors, and others. Dealing with crisis and trauma is not for the fainthearted. Regardless of one's stamina and adaptability, time and exposure deposit layers of stress that are not easily shaken off and often results in dysfunction.

Chapter 4
Internal Alchemy

Internal alchemy focuses on changing energies and substances within the human condition. The practices focus on restoring balance and elevating vitality. The goals of internal alchemy are enlightenment, improved health, longevity, and peacefulness.

Energy diminishes during crisis and it conflicts with normal healthy body functions like breathing, heart rhythm, energy levels, decision-making, ability to respond quickly (e.g., to think on one's feet), and other psychological responses or behaviors that during a stressful or traumatic event are necessary for police, first responders and emergency workers.

1. <u>Steps to Reduce and Prevent Negative Outcomes</u>.

What can be done to address stress and adversity that are encountered by an organization's employees? Dependence on individual discipline or strict adherence to policy does not always provide the best outcome when a problem is discovered. There are current methods in use and they include:

A. Training and professional development. Not often required of every employee are topics areas that help an individual understand how stress and adversity can impact job performance. They include:

   1. Living a healthy lifestyle
   2. Health related oversight programs
   3. Duty related warning signs of stress
   4. Intervention and follow-up to traumatic events
   5. Warning systems that alert when stress is present
   6. Accountability to duty as a tool to manage oneself
   7. Learning resilience to moderate stress, adversity and trauma
   8. Steps to address employee needs and reduce the impact of stress

B. Supervisor Responsibility to Address Performance Manifestations.

   1. What is the key focus and why it must change.

   2. Knowledge in observing, identifying and addressing dysfunction.

   3. Overseeing the individual with a problem.

      a) Recognition that an issue exists and that action is necessary.
      b) First contact with the individual is important and the manner in which the discussion is initiated must be with care and sensitivity to the individual.
      c) Establishing communications; do so in person and at a time that is convenient to the individual.

d) Fact finding is critical as all relevant information must be known and used to make decisions. Do not gloss over or hope you have it right. Be sure.

e) Establishing a plan and eliciting compliance is done with the individual and should not occur without collaboration between supervisor and employee. No buy-in will be achieved if the person you are working with feels isolated.

f) Developing a plan leads to implementation. This stage is important and must include a timeframe for all parties involved.

g) Monitor and coach and do not think that once a plan is implemented that it will work as designed. Collect information and pay attention. Keep your communications with the individual at the forefront.

h) Path to wellness is fraught with speed bumps. Work to minimize them.

i) Once the change effort is over, prevent slippage and encourage growth.

2. Aspects of Durability:

Individual endurance consists of numerous skills and abilities that a person can use as strategies to assist in recovering from stress, adversity or trauma. Understanding what endurance is enables us to build a reservoir of strengths that we can draw on when faced with a situation that is difficult, stressful and requires personal fortitude and endurance. Endurance can be described as the measure of a person's stamina or persistence.

A. The power to adapt to adversity.

- When everything around you is in chaos, you are able to see clearly and assess the situation, leading to decisions that are appropriate and provide a safer position, which eventually points the way to recovery.

- You understand that a return to the normal that was present before the event is probably not possible. But you are determined to overcome the issues, determine next steps, and make the necessary changes.

B. To manage stress, grief, and adversity.

- When others are fleeing or hunkering down, withdrawn and not accepting that an incident has happened, you begin an assessment to understand what has happened and what can be done to move forward.

- While experiencing worry and concern you continue to function and to map out positive changes.

C. To return in a planned way to renewed personal balance, productivity, and well-being in life.

- Realizing that there are no guarantees in life, you accept that personal balance is a matter of vision and reality allowing you adapt to the current situation and move forward.

- Forging a plan that addresses the major barriers allows the individual to find balance in what must be done and reduces a confused and unproductive effort.

D. To reduce negativity, anger and other maladies that disrupts normal life.

- One of the first steps is to recognize that maladies are present and to acknowledge they are not normal and can be combated.

- The second step is to determine what can be done to change things, turn them around and begin recovery.

E. Promotes regaining control of your life as it relates to family, friends, work, community and other commitments.

- Create a new vision for yourself. Cast aside the burden you have shouldered and accept that change is possible, will happen, and set your mind to beginning that climb back to emotional and physical health.

- Include those others with whom a more balanced lifestyle is desired.

- Provide personal skills and leadership when the situation presents itself and you are able to contribute.

3. Using Durability Techniques to Moderate Negative Outcomes

Strengthening durability, resiliency and personal grit should not be left to experience resulting from encounters on the street. The old adage "tough it out" may sound good in the locker room but it does not serve justice when the result of exposure to continuous trauma leaves the individual stressed and suffering all manner of manifestation. Police and first responders should receive training that begins in the academy that is designed to meet the needs of the individual, his or her organization and the larger community, to address encounters with adversity, trauma and life changing events. Such a program specifically addresses teaching police and first responder requisite skills to appropriately handle personal, departmental and community adversity and stress inducing events.

It is no less important than other types of training to strengthen a person's resolve and prepare them to reduce the harmful effects of job related stress. Training provides individuals with the ability to manage stressful situations, adversity and trauma by overcoming issues and problems and to emerge without lasting negative effects. The constant threat of danger, potential for injury, unsafe situations, death, hazardous encounters, required engagement in events that others avoid and numerous other stress inducing situations, leads to numerous physiological, psychological and sociological issues.

The list of negative outcomes includes frayed emotions, anger, impatience, divorce rates that are twice that of the general population, high rates of suicide, alcohol and substance abuse, high risk lifestyle, intimacy problems, and aberrant behavior. When stress catches up, we often observe disciplinary issues occurring. Supervisors are aware that change has happened, but often do not address underlying causes resorting to threat, warning or discipline as treatment. Not only does the individual suffer, it has an equally negative Impact on family, friends and colleagues. In addition, work performance generally diminishes. Over time these individual's suffer loss of a balanced life and find they are narrowly defining the world around them. The gradual accumulation of stress and adversity will, over time, contribute to physical and mental health issues that include respiratory, heart, over-weight, back trouble, higher mortality cancer, anger issues, substance abuse, promiscuous behavior, elevated risk taking, relationship problems, lack of humor, suspicion of people factor, and other issues. Seeing the worst that society can offer and the accompanying tragedy takes its toll.

Police and first responder officials additionally experience the pressure of constantly being on-guard and anticipating extreme situations. For fire fighters, it is the inherent danger of building or car fires with lethal chemicals, explosion and structurally unsafe structures. Police encounters can turn violent and life-threatening with no warning. There is the constant pressure of dealing with people and issues that are difficult to resolve. Correctional officers work in close proximity with inmates, whose behavior can turn deadly with little to no provocation, raising stress levels to their highest rating even when everything is seemingly calm. Emergency management, emergency medical and a host of other agency specialties have numerous examples of inherent and associated danger that over time leads to stress and related illnesses.

We are by nature resilient people, able to step up and meet adversity with courage, inner strength, and determination to resolve problems. There are times when extraordinary or persistent issues occupy our thinking, leaving us anxious, angry, frustrated, and with other accompanying emotions. A person with grit has the ability to recover from and adjust to misfortune, disaster, or undue change by drawing on internal strengths and abilities, forging a positive outlook, managing strong feelings and impulses, and ultimately solving the problem.

The ability to manage and diminish the effects of adversity and trauma is critical to physical and mental wellness, well-being, and a balanced lifestyle. Understanding the factors of resilience and strategies for strengthening our ability to withstand extraordinary and high risk situations results in improved life-balance, ability to assist others, and fulfill the expectations and obligations associated with one's job, organization and community service.

Police and first responder personnel and agencies must address the cumulative effects of encountering violence, dysfunction, catastrophic events and numerous other stress producing incidents that are prevalent within the duties and service role of this occupational group. Resilience skills are an integral component of planning in life and used to oppose and reduce "risk factors" that threaten or endanger a person, an organization, or a community's well-being and security. The ability to withstand pressure, to react with confidence, and to effectively continue to carry out one's duties, while others are incapacitated, emerges from a person's inner resilience.

4. Fourteen Points to Strengthen Durability[28]:

Identify issues that are harmful, what to do about them, and strategies that might work for you.

Issue	Understanding and Awareness
1. Learning skills to address stress and adversity. Health issues.	The **"Strengthening Durability and Personal Grit"** training program for police and first responders officials is designed to meet the needs of individuals, organizations and community to address encounters with adversity, trauma and life changing events. This program specifically addresses teaching police and first responder officers' skills to appropriately handle personal, departmental and community adversity and stress inducing events. Long-term exposure to negative events and situations is harmful to physical and mental health. The nature of the work performed is fraught with all manner of human misery and harm. A human being is capable of love and cruelty and it is the cruel acts inflicted on others to which our first responders go and encounter deviant and inflicted harm that is sometimes difficult to reconcile. Over a period of years we may find ourselves immune to what we witness, but it imprints in our psyche, adding to the darkness of thought and, sometimes action. It manifests itself with changes in our behavior. We may get angry quicker or find our tolerance to situations frayed thin. Suspicion, lack of trust, caution and a wait and watch attitude when meeting people, leads to further isolation, much of it within our own heads. It is harmful and has deleterious effect on those others who share our lives; family, work, friends, and associates. We can work through it, not twenty years from now, but as a parallel wellness approach to work and life. Like treating a physical illness, we must address the psychological as well as bodily harm, the two being mutually entwined and inseparable.
2. Self-management techniques to overcome job related stress and trauma	No less important than other types of training, "Strengthening Resolve and Durability" can help reduce harmful effects of job related stress. Training provides individuals with the ability to manage stressful situations, adversity and trauma by overcoming issues and problems and to emerge without lasting negative effects. The constant threat of danger, potential for injury, unsafe situations, death, hazardous encounters, requires engagement in events that others avoid. Numerous other stress inducing situations leads to various physiological, psychological and sociological issues.

---

[28] Adapted by Lumb to this text from earlier work on the topic of resilience.

	Particularly in youth, we believe we are invincible, tough and able to survive to whatever may come our way. That is not a bad attitude, for fortitude begins within. Self-management can be assisted with supervisor attentiveness and care. Aware that acts of inhumanity imprint on the mind and subtly shove normalcy to the side, we must also acknowledge that years of these events soon take up substantial space both consciously and subconsciously. We must not allow ourselves to blindly move forward believing in the myth of invincibility. We need to learn of the many ways to help ourselves and, when necessary, to help others as well.
3. What we see with stressed individuals.	Negative emotions, anger, impatience, divorce rates that are twice that of the general population, high rate of suicide, alcohol and substance abuse, high risk lifestyle, intimacy problems, and aberrant behavior top the list of negative symptoms. This has a negative Impact on family, friends and colleagues and impacts work performance. Durability training provides tools that assist individuals in finding balance in their lives. If our employee, peer or colleague will not accept that changes are happening, what to do about it? Generally, we wait for their return and/or hope for the best, generally saying, "Ole Paul, give him some time and he will be okay!" Perhaps or perhaps not! It is not easy to step up to the plate and confront an employee, friend or fellow colleague, but it is preferable to ignoring the situation until the meltdown occurs or the individual finally does something to hurtle him or herself over the cliff. Suggestions and methods to approach and assist someone are available. Reference is made to an earlier published resource for this purpose: Breazeale, R., & Lumb, R. (2013), *Building Resilience: Peer Coaching Manual*. Amazon Publishing.
4. Physical, psychological & emotional harm	The gradual accumulation of stress will, over time, contribute to physical and mental health issues that include respiratory, heart, obesity, back trouble, higher mortality cancer, anger issues, substance abuse, promiscuous behavior, elevated risk taking, relationship problems, lack of humor, suspicion of people factor, and other issues. Working for years in high stress occupations often results is a diminishing life style, attitude, humor, and health. Seeing the worst that society can offer, and the accompanying tragedy, takes its toll. We expect changes in our physical and mental functions as we age, but when hastened by exposure to work related trauma, understanding that it is happening is the first step. Not easy for any of us to consider that perhaps, just perhaps, we are collecting images and experiences that can be harmful to our physical,

	psychological and emotional well-being. With awareness comes realization that we can do something positive to counteract the outcome of negativity, but it first requires a willing attitude to do so.
5. The environment of danger and accumulating discouragement	Police and first responder officials additionally experience the pressure of constantly being on-guard and anticipating extreme situations. For fire personnel it is the inherent danger of fire with lethal chemicals, explosion and buildings that are structurally unsafe. Police encounters can turn violent and life-threatening with no warning. There is constant pressure of dealing with people and issues that are difficult to resolve. Emergency management, correctional officers, emergency medical and a host of other agency specialties have numerous examples of inherent and associated danger that, over time, leads to stress and related illnesses. The work environment is quite predictable since the same events have happened for decades, in different situations, involving different people and victims, but with similar outcomes. Murder is murder whether in the first century or the 21st century. Carnage is carnage regardless. Dealing with it then were people like us. This knowledge can be helpful when combined with a statement like, "You will encounter the following situations. When they are over, here are things you must do to self-help and things the organization must do to assist you in this step. We must not allow it to be ignored, for it is a weakness in today's world, and we are not doing enough prevention and strengthening our employees with resilience and endurance skills, knowledge and attitude building.
6. Addressing harmful high risk job situations	Police and first responder personnel and agencies must address the cumulative effects of encountering violence, dysfunction, catastrophic events and numerous other stress producing incidents that are prevalent within the duties and service role of this occupational group. Durability skills are an integral component of planning in life and used to oppose and reduce "risk factors" that threaten or endanger a person, an organization, or a community's well-being and security. The ability to withstand pressure, to react with confidence, and to effectively continue to carry out one's duties, while others are incapacitated, emerges from a person's inner durability. It begins with acknowledgement that what we see and encounter is not normal to most of society, yet in doing our jobs we will find ourselves immersed and cannot easily walk away. That awareness allows us to take follow-up steps to put the event into perspective and rescue our thoughts from negativity to optimism.
7. Calling on personal grit to overcome	We are, by nature, durable and resilient people who are able to step up and meet adversity with courage, inner strength, and determination to resolve problems. There are times when

adversity	extraordinary or persistent issues occupy our thinking, leaving us anxious, angry, frustrated, and with other accompanying emotions. A person with grit has the ability to recover from and adjust to misfortune, disaster, or undue change by drawing on internal strengths and abilities, forging a positive outlook, managing strong feelings and impulses, and ultimately solving the problem. While it sounds contrite, we are capable of turning our thoughts from negativity to a more positive focus. Our thinking will often take its own direction without our conscious permission. A young person, lying in bed at night, the room dark, and he or she imagines there is something under the bed. The thought builds and fear emerges, the body becomes still, hearing is acute, sounds magnified and the slightest movement amplified. Flight is possible, crying out another reaction or remaining still until sleep takes over and we wake in the morning, all memories erased.
8. What is a balanced lifestyle? Turning the corner.	The ability to manage and diminish the effects of adversity and trauma are critical to physical and mental wellness, well-being, and a balanced lifestyle. Understanding the factors of durability and strategies for strengthening our ability to withstand extraordinary and high risk situations results in improved life-balance, ability to assist others, and fulfill the expectations and obligations associated with one's job, organization and community service. Several strategies are offered in this book and reference is made to those sections. What feels right for you probably is. The next issue, number 9, is a strategy that has worked for others as well. Selecting one or two that feel right for you and writing down what you think they mean and how they can work for you, helps to ground them for personal use when needed.
9. Strategies for change.	Key strategies to strengthen personal Durability and coping skills include: • Establish and map out strategies to achieve goals. • Maintain open communications with family and friends. • Acknowledge that change is normal and that adaptation is possible. • When confronting crisis you are confident in bringing it under control. • Maintain a positive view of yourself and trust in your instinct and ability. • Be decisive in your actions and address problems in a straightforward manner. • Manage your outlook, be optimistic, and visualize where you want to be and how to get there. • Take care of your physical and mental health by managing stress and engaging in activities that you enjoy and that are

	relaxing. • Establishment of a strong peer coaching program in organizations with sufficient back-up resources to maintain an effective program is critical.
10. Protecting <u>internal</u> body systems	We take exceptional care to outfit our police and first responder officers with all manner of equipment and tools to protect their physical well-being. We do not provide skills and tools that are equally powerful in protecting the psychological and emotional well-being of our personnel. Durability training assists in addressing this issue in a planned and thorough manner. The challenge is to make this a primary goal of the organization, a routine and mandated step that is as important as the other tools we need to do the job.
11. Addressing job cultural inhibitors. Demanding change.	More must be done due to the culture and isolation that eventually takes place among our first responder community. 1. One of the suggestions, as an outcome of this training, is to suggest that you take the lead and form a discussion group within your agency. This group will form the core of individuals interested in promoting emotional health, undertake planning to address issues, and educate themselves on the effects of stress, adversity and trauma as it affects life-style, health, work performance and relationships. 22. Education and knowledge can lead to the formation of a sophisticated program that is designed to help fellow officers who are experiencing stress and other debilitating pressure. 33. It will not be easy given the culture and the protective silence that officers or first responders wrap themselves in. If you review history, we have lost a lot of good men and women because of the effect of accumulated stress, resulting in dysfunction and the onset of problems.

12.
Don't wait for someone else to set the standard, you do it!
	Organize a peer emotional health help group.
	
	1. Schedule a "Building Durability meeting in a place offering comfort and privacy.
	2. Have refreshments available.
	3. Have a designated facilitator (can/should be one of your group).
	4. Have an agenda that list one or two items.
	    a) General discussion of stress and encountering adversity
	    b) List steps to reduce and lessen the effects and ask if anyone will discuss if they have used any of them.

	5. Schedule a second meeting and select one of the 'Building Durability" topics that the group will discuss and explore how it can be applied using specific examples from past encounters.
	Note: Police and first responder organizations should host similar meetings that are held informally and with the purpose of addressing stress, adversity and strenuous conditions and calls.
13. Employees leading the charge. Taking responsibility for self and peers.	Employees can also conduct meetings and develop a program that is focused on the needs of those who are experiencing high levels of stress and emotional dysfunction. Employee meetings should take place in an informal and comfortable environment leading to a discussion about emotional and performance issues and concerns that are more often than not ignored and buried while still alive in one's psyche. The emotional and psychological health of employees are being discussed in a non-threatening and information gathering session. Solutions will emerge to existing problems if the group is tenacious and long-standing.
14. Overcoming personal trauma	This discussion provides an overview of the effects of stress and adversity and presents techniques and strategies to help overcome personal trauma. It is all for naught if left on the shelf and ignored. Like physical health and well-being, it is our conscious effort to remain well that allows a visit to a doctor for an annual physical, to eat right, to not ignore warning signs that something is not right, etc. These same needs surround our emotional and psychological balance. Do not ignore this aspect of your being. To do so is to invite disaster.

Another list, provided by the American Psychological Association[29] offers "Ten ways to build resilience" that are helpful to consider. They are stated as taken from the website, referenced below.

1. Make connections. Good relationships with close family members, friends or others are important. Accepting help and support from those who care about you and will listen to you strengthens resilience. Some people find that being active in civic groups, faith-based organizations, or other local groups provides social support and can help with reclaiming hope. Assisting others in their time of need also can benefit the helper.

2. Avoid seeing crises as insurmountable problems. You can't change the fact that highly stressful events happen, but you can change how you interpret and respond to these events. Try looking beyond the present to how future circumstances may be a

---

[29] http://www.apa.org/helpcenter/road-resilience.aspx#

little better. Note any subtle ways in which you might already feel somewhat better as you deal with difficult situations.

3. Accept that change is a part of living. Certain goals may no longer be attainable as a result of adverse situations. Accepting circumstances that cannot be changed can help you focus on circumstances that you can alter.

4. Move toward your goals. Develop some realistic goals. Do something regularly — even if it seems like a small accomplishment — that enables you to move toward your goals. Instead of focusing on tasks that seem unachievable, ask yourself, "What's one thing I know I can accomplish today that helps me move in the direction I want to go?"

5. Take decisive actions. Act on adverse situations as much as you can. Take decisive actions, rather than detaching completely from problems and stresses and wishing they would just go away.

6. Look for opportunities for self-discovery. People often learn something about themselves and may find that they have grown in some respect as a result of their struggle with loss. Many people who have experienced tragedies and hardship have reported better relationships, greater sense of strength even while feeling vulnerable, increased sense of self-worth, a more developed spirituality and heightened appreciation for life.

7. Nurture a positive view of yourself. Developing confidence in your ability to solve problems and trusting your instincts helps build resilience.

8. Keep things in perspective. Even when facing very painful events, try to consider the stressful situation in a broader context and keep a long-term perspective. Avoid blowing the event out of proportion.

9. Maintain a hopeful outlook. An optimistic outlook enables you to expect that good things will happen in your life. Try visualizing what you want, rather than worrying about what you fear.

10. Take care of yourself. Pay attention to your own needs and feelings. Engage in activities that you enjoy and find relaxing. Exercise regularly. Taking care of yourself helps to keep your mind and body primed to deal with situations that require resilience.

Summary Statement.

Stress and adversity are natural outcomes of work and other life events. When employment is within high stress parameters, employees need ways to reduce the negativity before it adversely impacts health. Denial is a powerful motivator to tough it out, but research tells us that we are seldom successful. The key is to engage in stress reduction activities, something that is pleasurable, or that allows for positive or healthy outlets for ones thoughts and feelings, will help to curb pressures and balance life events and engagements.

Fourteen ways to strengthen durability to deal with stress, adversity and trauma were offered. The selection offers something for everyone. The key is to find one or more that feels right, to learn how to use them in one's personal quest for well-being. This can be done in conjunction with others, by oneself, and certainly through organized programs within the workplace. Understand yourself, learn more about issues experienced and determine what will work to make life improve. You need not go this alone, for you are not! Knowing this allows a more open approach to find solutions to those things that are troubling.

Additionally, the American Psychological Association's ten ways to build resilience are of value. They should be considered against one's life circumstance and to help determine if one or more of the offered resilience building tips can be applied to one's life or that of a family member, friend, colleague, or others.

APA: http://www.apa.org/helpcenter/road-resilience.aspx

Chapter 5
A New Dimension: Suicide by Cop

Addressing the Aftermath of Suicide by Cop: Managing Post Event Consequences Experienced by Police and Other Responders[30]

Chapter Co-Author
  Gary Metz, Associate Professor
    State University of New York at Brockport

I. Introduction.

In the past several years, we have all become more aware that the media and general public believe that some individuals want the police to kill them, to end their life, carrying out an action they are unable to do themselves. This situation has been labeled as *"suicide by cop"* (*SbC*), a term that somehow captures the image that this is a general service our police provide for people with suicide ideology, but who lack personal courage to carry out the final act themselves. That image or belief is far from the truth and reality of each situation. Still, the seeming simplicity of the act makes it appealing to some individuals who choose to die, notwithstanding the indignity of asking (or forcing) police to terminate life needlessly.

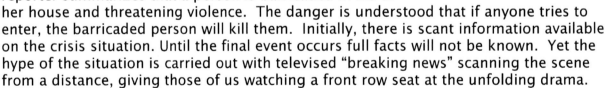

An image of police with rifles, tactical gear and an established protective perimeter, designated by yellow tape, is broadcast on the local news channel. A breathless reporter summarizes that a person is barricaded in his or her house and threatening violence. The danger is understood that if anyone tries to enter, the barricaded person will kill them. Initially, there is scant information available on the crisis situation. Until the final event occurs full facts will not be known. Yet the hype of the situation is carried out with televised "breaking news" scanning the scene from a distance, giving those of us watching a front row seat at the unfolding drama.

The situation ends when an aggressive act causes an exchange of gun fire and the suspect lies dead. The perfunctory statements are made, "*It will be investigated by the Attorney General's Office!*" and "*A report will be forthcoming when the investigation is complete.*" To most casual observers it is the end of the story, and unless the individual was personally known, the incident is quickly forgotten in this world of rapidly changing, fast breaking news.

In reality, the described incident is a deeply social concern that began at the finish line (when the event, the shooting, occurred) for those involved. The real story

---

[30] 2011 files/publishing/ book /chapter suicide by cop

excludes the many life events of the deceased prior to the 911 call and the arrival of the police, EMTs and other first responders. All manner of fact will later be discovered and recorded from the post-incident investigation. Questions will be posed seeking to bring a more clear understanding. What were the contributing factors to someone establishing a combat situation that involved the police? What mental health, or substance abuse, or personal life stressors were present that had developed over time? What was being done along this continuum that failed to achieve desired outcomes of reducing stress and to improve functioning and quality of life? What could have been done to realize a more successful outcome? And, importantly, how many others had critical information or important knowledge before the police were called and failed to take appropriate action to mitigate the situation?

Collaboration between Public Safety, First Responders and others with important roles is the key to successful outcomes of serious situations.

Seldom is a situation as the one described above spontaneous, meaning that it suddenly occurred with no warning. There are indicators, experiences, situations and quantifiable examples that lead to the conclusion that the individual substantially changed (toward the negative with mood, affect, behavior, etc.) over time. Worry, fear, concern, paranoia—all lead to an unwillingness to engage in prevention and are all too common in situations like this. Sadly, when the final event occurs, we often hear, *"I wish I had . . .",* but it is too late!

Not every outcome is preventable. However, there are milestones along a path of dysfunction, change and decline where appropriate intervention may have changed the outcome. Police and first responders enter when the last act is about to be played out. By then, choices are few. This leads one to consider how society and individuals might address these types of concerns long before options, if any remain, run out.

We define *"suicide by cop"* as a suicidal person provoking police, utilizing aggressive action and accompanying threat of violence, that result in police action resulting in the death of the individual (Dewey et al, 2013[31]). While the prevalence of this incident is unknown, there is also a lack of uniform definition, reporting and research to determine causation, occurrence and management of this type of call for service (Pinizzotto, Davis, & Miller, 2005[32]). More remains to be done to identify steps that police can use to reduce the outcome of death and to engage with the community in determining prevention steps. This is not just a police issue, it is a social concern and as such whole communities must engage in collaborative community building to reduce this type of incident.

---

[31] Lauren Dewey , Maureen Allwood , Joanna Fava , Elizabeth Arias , Anthony Pinizzotto & Louis Schlesinger (2013) Suicide by Cop: Clinical Risks and Subtypes, Archives of Suicide Research, 17:4, 448-461

[32] Pinizzotto, A. J., Davis, E. F., & Miller, C. E. (2005). Suicide by cop: Defining a devastating dilemma. FBI Law Enforcement Bulletin, 74(2), 8-20.

Police response to calls for service always carries the threat of danger, with each call harboring its own demands, needs and solutions. Forced into a life or death situation, even if feigned, must never result in hesitation and harm to the officer. The officer provides a role that the general population does not fully understand and they trained in this role (to protect and serve in potentially life-threatening situations). The public's mindset is that the police are at our disposal, paid for by our taxes. The public want police to provide these services, and are willing to pay someone (i.e., police) to do it for them. The choice is clear and when the officer is threatened, he or she must initiate protective measures. Protecting themselves and others from harm, even when personal danger is present, is an ever present obligation. Never does the officer report for duty with the hope of engaging in deadly force. The tenuousness of life should not reach the level of involving others to engage in action they do not want to perform, but due to circumstance, alternatives are few, if any exist at all.

Whether true or misleading, misunderstanding improperly labels a complex situation as something it may not be. When the level of threat and risk are high, police respond with a plan and their training and experience provide guidance on managing outcomes. The higher the level of danger, the more police will engage a higher level of elevated safety procedures. These include specialty response protocols and employ a more progressive pace, involve seeking additional information, weighing options, taking control of the situation and pursuing the best possible resolution. Time slows down, command and control dominate, and resolution is sought with a minimum use of force. Patience must rule. Through careful training and from a very thorough and rapid assessment of the situation, a measured and planned response can occur. Despite training, experience and this careful planning, deadly force may result. Obviously, it is typically not recommended as the first course of action.

Consideration of collaboration with agencies or groups possessing needed expertise to assist with complex situations is encouraged. This action is not always a natural response, as police concerned with safety and scene control may exclude other service engagement, even if it can assist in achieving desired outcomes. While not always possible, we know that a collaboration model can make a substantial difference.

We are referring here to the collaboration and/or planning intervention with Emergency Medical Services, mental health, negotiation, crisis counseling, and expertise in information search and analysis. Dewey et al, (2013) acknowledges that this is not just a police problem for it also includes other providers, specifically mental health, substance abuse and those who provide assessment, intervention and partnership on sustainable problem solving.

II. Studies of Interest to Enhance Understanding.

Understanding the motivation behind a person wanting to die and not having the courage to take their own life may help a police officer comprehend the how and why of this encounter. Death by cop most often results in feelings of deep grief, confusion, guilt, among other emotions. Coming to terms with this type of police situation requires time, energy and its own level of skilled support and intervention as the officer moves through a very intense response to a very abnormal and potentially avoidable situation.

Minimizing guilt is important, as the duty of a police officer often takes them into harm's way, where quick decisions must be made and action taken may result in second guessing or defense of having to do what they did. In any case, it is difficult for the officer and contributing to their well-being is equally important.

Earlier studies (Hutson et al., 1998[33]; Kennedy et al., 1998[34]; Lord, 1998[35], 2010; Parent and Verdun-Jones, 1998[36]; Wilson et al., 1998[37]) support the conclusion that at least 10% of police deadly force incidents involve suicide by cop situations. Homant et al. (1999)[38] reviewed 123 cases of what has been referred to as 'suicide by cop'. In 56% of these incidents, police or others were wounded, in 22% the suspect merely bluffed some sort of threat and in 22% a more ambiguous level of danger was present.

Review of 123 Cases of Suicide by Cop Incidents

56 percent	Police of others wounded
22 percent	The suspect bluffed a threat taken seriously by the officers
22 percent	The level of danger was present but not apparent initially

Best et al (2004[39]) posed the following nine questions, grouped into <u>four categories</u> that help explain the phenomenon of Suicide by Cop and can lead to training revision, establishment of collaborative partnerships for response and a change in action determination. Lord & Sloop (2010) used eleven slightly modified categories in their research.

Table 1.
Primary indicators of suicidal intent

---

[33] Hutson, H. R., Anglin D., Yarbrough J., Hardaway K., Russell M., Strote J., Canter M., & Blum, B. (1998). Suicide-By-Cop. *Annals of Emergency Medicine, 32*(6), 665-669

[34] Kennedy, D. B., Homant, R. J., & Hupp, R. T. (1998, August). Suicide-By-Cop. *FBI Law Enforcement Bulletin*, 21-27.

[35] Lord, V. B. (1998). One form of victim-precipitated homicide: The use of law enforcement officers to commit suicide. Paper presented at the annual meeting of the Academy of Criminal Justice Sciences.

[36] Parent, R. B. & Verdun-Jones, S. (1998). Victim-precipitated homicide: Police use of deadly force in British Columbia. *Policing: An International Journal of Police Strategies and Management, 21*, 432-448.

[37] Wilson, E. F., Davis, J. H., Bloom, J. D., Batten, P. J., & Kamara, S. G. (1998, January). Homicide or suicide: The killing of suicidal persons by law enforcement officers. *Journal of Forensic Sciences, 43*, 46-52.

[38] Homant, R. J., Kennedy, D. B., & Hupp, R. T. (2000). Real and perceived danger in police officer assisted suicide. Journal of Criminal Justice, 28, 43-52

[39] Besta, D., Quigley A., & Bailey, A. (2004). Police shooting as a method of self-harming: A review of the evidence for 'suicide by cop' in England and Wales between 1998 and 2001. International Journal of the Sociology of Law Sociology of Law, 32 (2004) 349-361.

Lord, V. & Sloop, M. (2010)[40]	Best, D., Quigley, A. & Bailey, A. (2004)[41].
1. The individual is known to have explicitly communicated a suicidal intention during or before the incident (Communicated intent).	The nine questions, grouped into four categories are:
	A. Primary evidence of suicidal intent
2. The individual indicates nonverbal suicidal intent through life threatening and criminal behavior with a lethal weapon or what appears to be a lethal weapon (Showed intent).	1. Is the individual known to have explicitly communicated a suicidal intention during or immediately before the incident? (Communicated intent) or
3. The individual deliberately engineers contact with police either by direct telephone contact with police or use of an "outrageous act" (Planned contact). Secondary indicators of suicidal intent:	2. Did the individual deliberately engineer contact with armed police either by direct telephone contact with the police or by displaying the weapon in a police station? (Engineered contact)
4. The individual has a history of previous suicide attempts (Previous suicide attempts).	**B. Secondary indicators of suicidal intent**
	3. Did the individual have a history of previous suicide attempts? (Previous attempts)
5. The individual is confronted by officers immediately after committing an offense, or the subject is served a warrant. The individual threatens the officers with a weapon or threat of a weapon, stating he (she) would rather "die than go back to jail" (Criminal act). Evidence of irrational thought	4. Did the individual challenge officers with what they knew to be unloaded or replica weapons, in order to provoke them to shoot? (Unloaded or replica weapon)
	C. State-based indicators of irrationality (motive uncertain)
6. The individual's behavior is rendered significantly irrational as a consequence of alcohol or drug intoxication (Intoxicated).	5. Was their behavior rendered significantly irrational as a consequence of alcohol or drug intoxication? (Intoxicated)
7. The individual's behavior is irrational as a consequence of diagnosed mental health problems (Mental illness).	6. Was their behavior irrational as a consequence of diagnosed mental health problems? (Mental health)
8. The individual has a current history of substance abuse (Addiction).	7. Had the individual been involved in a domestic dispute immediately prior to

---

[40] Lord, V., & Sloop, M. (2010). Suicide by Cop: Police Shooting as a method of self-harming. Journal of Criminal Justice, 38, 889-895.
[41] Best, D., Quigley, A. & Bailey, A. (2004). Police shooting as a method of self-harming: A review of the evidence for suicide by cop in England and Wales between 1998 and 2001. International Journal of the Sociology of Law, 32, 349-361.

9. The individual has been involved in a domestic dispute or separation prior to the incident. Other precipitating events could include serious financial loss (Interpersonal crisis). Minimal evidence of suicidal intentions: 10. The individual refuses to give up his (her) weapons to armed police in situations where the possibility of escape was minimal (Refusal to surrender). 11. The individual possesses a criminal history of especially violent crimes (Criminal history). Note: Lord & Sloop do not use categories in their study.	the incident? (Domestic dispute) **D. Minimal evidence of suicidal intention** 8. Did the individual refuse to give up their weapons to armed police in situations where the possibility of escape was minimal? (Refuse give up weapon) 9. Did the individual engage in any kind of behavior that can be regarded as confronting armed police? (Confronted armed police)

The study by Lord & Sloop (2010: 894) determined the following risk factors contribute to a "*suicide by cop*") outcome.

> *The current research found support for a model that contains a number of risk factors; however, some level of the three primary indicators - (1) communicate intent, (2) showed intent, and/or (3) planned intent to be killed - are necessary to distinguish SbC from self-inflicted suicides; the other indicators were not significant.* <u>Note</u>: See article for details.

Clinical Risk Factors.

What are the predictors of a person seeking to use the police as a means of suicide? If known information were available, what might police want to know before engaging with an individual who is potentially suicidal and who is considering death by the hands of the police? It seems to make sense that we should create a list of caution references that help with early decision-making. The value is to use this information and determine how we might operationalize policy, training and application for response to actual incidents. Treating a call for disturbance (as is often the case with more serious potential always at the door) can become life-threatening quickly. Point being, no officer should make any assumptions, rather be very cautious in response to all calls.

We live in an information world, one where overload can be debilitating as well as helpful. The key is to determine what is needed, how it will be used, who has access and other definitive policies that work to maintain effectiveness through protection. Not an easy task, but if we are to see any positive changes, our thinking into realms such as these must take place and officials must engage collaboratively.

Consideration of the variety of indicators of suicide endangerment can help with training and response planning. Is there pre-officer arrival information available that might indicate a level of risk and allow officer preparation to the potential of elevated danger?

At the very least, responding officers should know what information exists about situations that have forced an officer into a shooting scenario. Greater understanding and awareness of prior cases, where deadly force is about to be used against them, can provide a more in-depth response protocol.

One remaining deficit is the availability of a master list of people who have engaged in one of more of the following situations:

- Prior violence
- Mental health issues,
- Substance abuse issues
- Known threats toward others
- Record of prior calls to the address or person
- Violent encounter with police who responded to earlier calls
- Prior arrests or contact that included an elevated in emotional outburst

The technological systems available today are capable to retrieve all know information and perform analysis based on specific logarithms to determine frequency, risk, danger, deviant attitude and other indicators that produce a warning to use caution and conduct more in-depth investigation, we will elevate the safety warning system. All tools must be used to help reduce dangerous outcomes, for that should be the goal of all people and organizations.

While confidentiality is important in principle, there are certain types of service calls where the protection personal information must be weighed against for the greater welfare of others. In the case of a police officer responding to a call for service, undisclosed information has resulted in elevated danger. Prevention beats aggressive action every time. The greater good is, to our way of thinking, the dominant factor.

Table 2.
Typology of Suicide by Cop Indicators

Indicators
1. A prior suicide attempt is one of the best predictors of eventual suicide success (Innamorait et al., 2008).
2. The majority (65-87%) of individuals who committed *SbC* verbally communicated suicidal intent prior to or during the incident (Mohandie, 2008).
3. Of the 256 individuals who committed *SbC* in the study of officer involved shootings (Mohandie, 2008)[42].   ➢ 55% gave verbal indication of suicide

---

[42] Mohandie, K., Meloy, J. R., & Collins, P. I. (2009). Suicide by cop among officer-involved shooting cases. Journal of Forensic Sciences, 54(2), 456-462.

➢ 38% specifically referenced the method of SbC.
➢ 14% left a suicide note with four notes specifically addressed the method of SbC.
4. Regardless of gender, psychiatric disorders, particularly mood and substance use disorders, are very common among individuals who commit suicide (Moscicki, 1995)[43].
5. Across *SbC* studies, 40-63% of individuals were reported to have met criteria for at least one mental illness, with chronic depression, bipolar disorder, and schizophrenia being the most common diagnoses (Mohandie et al., 2009; Lord, 2000).
6. Mohandie et al., 2009; Homant, R. J., Kennedy, D. B., & Hupp, R. T. 2000, offer the following information: ➢ 29% of those who committed *SbC* were prescribed psychotropic medications, ➢ 21% had a prior psychiatric hospitalization ➢ 21% were under the care of a mental health professional ➢ 33-65% of individuals had a history of substance abuse
7. Mohandie et al. (2009): ➢ 36-56% of individuals committing *SbC* were alcohol intoxicated ➢ 52-76% rates increased when other drugs are considered
8. Interpersonal loss and conflicts are also common precipitants of suicidal behaviors Pompili, (2011)[44]
9. 70% experienced recent interpersonal problems (Lord, 2000).
10. 20-30% had a recent break up with a romantic partner (Lord, 2000).
11. 16-39% domestic disputes and/or domestic violence were considered precipitating factors Lord, (Mohandie, Meloy, & Collins, 2009)
12. Legal problems are also risk factors for suicide (Foster, 2011)[45].
13. Mohandie, Meloy, & Collins, (2009): ➢ 51-70%) of individuals who committed SbC had a history of arrest ➢ 26-47% began with police responding to an alleged crime
14. Impending incarceration was identified as a precipitator to SbC, (Lord, 2000).

Homant, R. J., Kennedy, D. B., & Hupp, R. T. (2000), categorized 143 cases in their research into three types. Their typology contained the following grouping:

1. **Disturbed Intervention Group**. Of this group, (57%) were not trying to gain police attention, but their irrational and emotionally disturbed behaviors gained attention and the situation escalated until the officers believed them to be dangerous to others or they became acutely suicidal, engaging in behavior that ultimately provoked the police to kill them.

---

[43] , E. K. (1995). Epidemiology of suicidal behavior. Suicide and Life Threatening Behavior, 25(1), 22-35.

[44] Pompili, M., Innamorati, M., Szanto, K., Di Vittorio, C., Conwell, Y., Lester, D., & Amore, M. (2011). Life events as precipitants of suicide attempts among first-time suicide attempters, repeaters, and non-attempters. Psychiatry Research, 186(2-3), 300-305.

[45] Foster, T. (2011). Adverse life events proximal to adult suicide: A synthesis of findings from psychological autopsy studies. Archives of Suicide Research, 15(1), 1-15.

2. **Direct Confrontation Group**. Of this group 31% planned ahead of time to attack the police with the purpose of being killed.

3. **Criminal Intervention Group**. Of this group 12% were engaged in criminal activity without intent to gain police attention. When police arrived the perpetrators seemed to prefer death to arrest. Police intervention is unwelcome but the individual would rather be killed than be arrested.

There are implications that extend beyond the call for service. They go to elevating the response when the threat of danger is such that the officer's or other lives are at stake. This would also include the person who is the focus of police attention. At that moment of realization, the officer's actions and behavior revert to their training, acquiring a survival mode and automatic responses that emerge from academy training, experience and personal processing of what is being seen, heard and felt.

We must understand the whole mental process of suicide as a means to an end. What motivates someone to consider this life ending event and particularly individuals who are considering forcing police to carry out the means to their end? Suicide ideology culminating in a situation where death is anticipated is difficult to reconcile when compared to someone whose normal thinking is not considering this act. Accomplishing one's suicide utilizing another person is even more complex and far out of the norm of everyday living. The officers, who find themselves in this situation, are familiar with abnormal behavior of people they encounter, but the irrationality of this act is confounding at the least and horrifying to contemplate at its worst case scenario. Therefore, understanding the reasons why, and importantly, what the officer can do to both minimize and manage pre- and post-incidents is of value to personal emotional health and well-being.

1. Information. When dispatch has a name they must run a criminal history and name search to determine if the individual has had past contact with the police. A study by Dewey (2013)[46] determined that 66 percent of their sample had prior contact. Another area of importance is to seek information on mental health status, substance abuse and other factors that may point to a penchant for confrontation. All pre-arrival information should be immediately relayed to responding personnel.

When the inquiry by dispatch includes information of prior history indicating violence or the potential for it to occur, additional units must be dispatched immediately, and required by policy. Once engaged in a situation with a physical confrontation ensuing, timely action is required. It is easier to resume normal duty than engaging after the fact with negative outcomes.

2. Other Expertise. All calls where behavior is deemed irrational, including rage, threats, violence, the individual is distressed and certainly when firearms are present, officers and first responders must elevate to a higher level of caution and approach/intervention. Calling in other forms of expertise (mental health, negotiators, others who may offer assistance for a non-violent solution) is important and could possibly and positively alter the outcome of the encounter, if time allows.

---

[46] Dewey, L., Allwood, M., Fava, J., Arias, E., Pinizzotto, A. & Schlesinger, L. (2013). Suicide by Cop: Clinical Risks and Subtypes, Archives of Suicide Research, 17:4, 448-461.

Pre-arrangement and inter-agency agreements or Memorandums of Understanding (MOU) must be in place to insure that response is not only anticipated, but properly staffed to allow it to happen when the call goes out. When a call is placed and the response is, "*We are not properly staffed at the present time!*" – the service was just declared not useful. Collaborative and inter-government and private provider agreements are easy to determine and construct. – Such planning can only emerge through careful collaboration with the designated area agencies and individuals.

3. Response. Police mindset is logically on containment, enforcement, control, and resolution, with the understanding that they are authorized to use force, to take such action as is deemed necessary to keep themselves and citizens safe. Unless hostages are part of the equation, time becomes the most important tool to allow for more careful planning and intervention. Allowing the situation to calm, to establish contact and have someone trained to interact with the individual, conceivably leading to a positive outcome, thus averting a devastating catastrophe.

Generally, the officer's thinking, the situation, the environment and social conditions all equate to urgency versus taking sufficient time to be more thorough. All of these are variables to consider and clearly will impact the outcome. Training will insure that all parties involved with the call have the proper response and are systematically poised to act appropriately.

> **Police mindset is logically on containment, enforcement, control, and resolution with understanding they are authorized to use force, to take such action as necessary to keep themselves and citizens safe.**

4. Police Action. Police must act in self-defense mode when their life is being threatened and determine that harm is eminent. Deadly force, justifiable homicide by a police officer, can and does take place. In all cases there is extensive investigation, review by several bodies (agency, Attorney General, Medical Examiner, others) where the facts are examined and the decision of justification is eventually determined. While most police shootings are found justified, we must still consider the officer and his or her well-being, public opinion, potential law suits and media response. These situations are complicated, at the very least. With careful planning, policy, training and attention to detail, Investigations into deadly force will follow through to an appropriate end result.

In a short article written by Kevin Caruso at Suicide.org[47], he provides relevant information that helps to explain suicide by cop and facts behind this serious event.

Suicide by Cop

Suicide by Cop occurs when people want to die but do not want to kill themselves. So they put themselves in a position where a police officer is forced to shoot them. A suicide by cop incident is extremely dangerous to police officers because they never

---

[47] http://www.suicide.org/suicide-by-cop.html

know if the individual will try to kill them, too. Some suicidal individuals will point an empty gun at the police because they know that the police will shoot back in self-defense.

Yet others will have a loaded gun and will want to kill as many police officers as possible before they die. Most police officers who are involved in suicide by cop incidents suffer emotional difficulties afterwards, and sometimes even suffer from post-traumatic stress disorder. And some people who die from suicide by cop leave notes explaining their reasons for taking their actions, and sometimes they apologize to the officers.

In a study that was published in the Annals of Emergency Medicine, researchers analyzed data from the Los Angeles County Sheriff's Department. The researchers concluded that suicide by cop was surprisingly common and the number of incidents was rising.

Researchers studied data from 1987 through 1997 and found that:

- 11 percent of officer-involved shootings were suicide by cop incidents.
- 98 percent were male
- 39 percent had a history of domestic violence
- Many individuals abused alcohol and/or drugs
- Many individuals had a prior history of suicide attempts
- About 50 percent of the weapons used were loaded
- 17 percent used a toy or replica gun

Caruso offers some sage advice to those who are considering this scenario, but getting them to consider alternatives is extremely difficult if not impossible. He states:

- If you even have the slightest thought in your mind about dying from suicide by cop, you need to get treatment immediately.

- You probably have an untreated mental illness, like depression.

- Depression is the number one cause for suicide.

- Dying from suicide by cop endangers the life of officers as well as civilians, and it is always the wrong thing to do.

- Suicide is never the answer to any problem.

- Suicide by cop is never the answer to any problem.

- Please reach out for help if you have suicidal thoughts of any kind.

Author comment: While somewhat redundant, the information from Caruso helps expand our thinking and reinforces current knowledge.

And, to imprint information that may be useful to responding officers, directing their thinking beyond routine to consideration of alternatives, the following study and author comments are provided.

The Los Angeles County Sheriff's Department study used all of the following criteria as a means of identifying "suicide by cop" incidents[48].

1. Evidence of suicidal intent that might include:

   A. Written note stating a wish to die
   B. Recent verbal communication of a desire to die to friends or family and at times to officers
   C. Suicidal characteristics or behavior indicating suicidal intent (i.e. holding a firearm to one's head.)

2. Evidence that suicidal individuals specifically wanted officers to shoot them:

   A. Outright statements by the precipitators indicating they wanted officers to shoot them.
   B. Written or verbal communication to family or friends stating they wanted officers to shoot them.
   C. Refusal to drop their weapon when advised by officers to do so and then aiming their weapon at officers or civilians.

3. Evidence the precipitator possessed a lethal weapon or what appeared to be a lethal weapon.

   A. Records maintained of concealed carry permits, gun shop purchases and other sources must be examined immediately by dispatch personnel and relevant information transmitted to field units.

   B. It is important that we find ways to combine specific information that can be immediately accessed and transmitted to officers prior to their arrival at the scene. The separate services of agencies and self-contained record systems have a valid purpose, but, with the safety of police officers and civilians threatened, it should not be an inhibitor.

4. Evidence the precipitator intentionally escalated the encounter and provoked officers to shoot them in self-defense or to protect civilians.

   A. This is where training and protocol are critical. The situation will dictate actions by police or others and in many cases the time to react is micro-seconds. When time can be slowed down, options to resolution are expanded, obviously the primary goal of any encounter.

---

[48] . Pyers, L. (2001). Suicide by Cop - The Ultimate "Trap". FBI National Academy Associates Magazine, Volume 3, No. 4, (July/August). http://www.theppsc.org/Staff_Views/Pyers/suicide_by_cop.htm

III. Can Police Reduce the Incidence of Fatalities?

The police are the primary responders to incidents where a threat to public health and welfare exist. Many police response calls include the presence of firearms, alcohol or drugs, domestic violence, mental health issues or a continuation of a criminal enterprise. When assessment discloses that a potential violent encounter and high risk conditions exist, tactical intervention is deemed appropriate. Again, time and situation dictate action and in many situations the full extent of a situation is unknown. Officer's literally make decisions "on the fly" meaning their intake of the scene, the conditions, the behaviors of others and more subtle input through sensory stimulus, trigger automatic reactions, emerging from training and experience. We criticize officer responses and for many, who have never been in the same situation, consider their expertise inappropriate. It is not! We must have confidence in the officer's training and experience, as well as policy and rules, for to second guess is simply unacceptable—and unfair.

Previous instances of similar situations offer knowledge of appropriate response. What can be learned and used to address future incidents is critical. Pre-event planning should include the police department working closely with mental health providers, substance abuse treatment personnel, and other first responders, who can be summoned to the scene, if time allows. It therefore makes perfect sense to identify these individuals, engage in training so that officers and requested expertise understand roles and procedures and have had the opportunity to engage in training, before the need arises. Pre-incident training provides response protocols, command and control planning, information access to allow in-depth inquiry and data analysis to assist in decision-making.

Crisis Intervention Training (CIT) is a program that has a history of success. Mental health providers, police, corrections, EMTs, Fire Service and others, all of whom are at the scene of an incident should be versed on the interventions potentially considered for use in the situation at hand. Awareness of role and function and common responses can only happen if there is a commitment to train together and determine the value of collaboration. Review of past incidents, lessons learned, and needs and future preparation are part of the collaboration and communication that must take place. Not to do so is to invite dysfunction and separate actions, neither of which work toward collective unification.

The evaluation of NAMI Maine's "Crisis Intervention Training" (CIT) program, for the period 2005-2007, by The Center for Health Policy, Planning and Research, at the University of New England (2007:4-6) divulged the following outcomes, which can be transposed to a model where many first responders work collaboratively to acquire similar outcomes.

The main findings of the evaluation regarding participation in the training include:

- Before attending CIT training, Maine correctional officers generally did not feel they had received adequate training in crisis intervention. This problem is made worse because jails do not consistently have adequate staffing or staff skilled in working with inmates' mental health and substance abuse problems, and community resources to assist staff and inmates are not readily available to the jails.

- Support from NAMI before, during, and after the training helped CIT officers and supervisors at the jails overcome some of the difficulties they faced in implementing CIT.

- Officers generally found the CIT training sessions to be useful in broadening their understanding of mental illness and substance abuse issues. They appreciated the opportunity to hear from family members of people with mental illness or substance abuse disorders at the CIT training and suggested expanded opportunities for role playing in future trainings.

- After attending the training, corrections officers reported a higher degree of comfort when encountering people with signs of mental illness, more confidence in their own ability to recognize maladaptive behaviors (including aggression) caused by mental illness, and more confidence to defuse or de-escalate situations as they arose. Officers also reported increased preparedness to handle people with mental illness in crisis, including those threatening to commit suicide. They were also more positive about their department's role in addressing mental health crises and had become more familiar with community resources.

- Officers who volunteered to attend the training tended to gain more knowledge and better understanding of CIT issues after attending the training compared to those who were mandated to attend. However, key informant interviews indicated that there is value in providing training to officers of all temperaments, background, and interest levels.

- The opportunity for correctional officers to gain awareness about mental health issues with members of law enforcement was a valuable and beneficial component of the training that provided important networking opportunities for both groups.

- Between May 2006 and August 2007, 162 CIT incidents were reported by participating county jail sites. There did not appear to be a correlation between the size of the jail and number of incidents reported. Although the number of trained officers at each site increased over time, the number of events observed did not appear to have increased over time. Instead, the incident rate peaked during some months.

- Approximately one quarter of CIT incidents involved at least one type of inmate aggression. Anger towards others, yelling and causing unrest, resisting instructions to comply, spitting, and throwing feces and urine on correctional staff are examples of aggression. To control the situations, officers were more likely to use force during instances of inmate aggression and verbal de-escalation techniques when inmates did not exhibit aggression.

- Inmates requiring CIT interventions are more likely to have preexisting mental illness and/or substance abuse problems. More than two thirds of the incidents included inmates with at least one mental health condition and almost two thirds of CIT incidents involved an inmate with at least one type of substance abuse problem.

- The most CIT incidents resulted in a mental health referral to a provider or community service.

- Some injuries occurred during CIT reported incidents. Of the 13 injuries sustained by inmates, 5 required medical attention. Of the 3 reported injuries to officers, 2 required medical attention.

IV. Summary and Recommendations.

There are numerous research studies that have examined the phenomenon of a police shooting as "*suicide by cop.*"

In hindsight, following the post-event investigation, we identify benchmarks that were indicators where intervention and prevention may have been successful. Questions often ask if alcohol, substance abuse, mental health issues, unstable job/unemployment, financial, domestic situations, anger and a history of other relevant incidents were present. Without broad agency access to that information, our approach to the situation is problematic, hampering the ability to make sustainable decisions on actions we can take. If this information were known, would the actual incident have been preventable if someone was able to sort it out and alternative actions were able to be taken?

Starting at the finish line, the incident that brought the police is not where we begin to determine "why" events unfurled as they did. We must look back at those individual episodes, indicators of "encounter risk," and use that information to formulate future response plans.

A summary of existing research will lead to a review of existing policy and training and suggest potential change in the following aspects:

- ➢ Collaborative situational response by public safety and first responders
- ➢ At scene action (data gathering, analysis, decision-making)
- ➢ Collaborative decision-making (if time allows)
- ➢ Implementation of a plan of action based on best practices and informed choice.
- ➢ Post-event evaluation and data gathering

Suicide by cop is a coined term to explain why some individuals confront police with the expectation that they will die. It is more common than statistics demonstrate, yet it carries post-event implications to the officer's well-being from that point forward (not to mention the ripple effect impacting the deceased individual and their family/friends). None-the-less, we must treat this event with the seriousness it deserves for it puts the unsuspecting police officer and other responders in situations with lasting negative consequences.

It is critical that we understand the issues, contributors, and facts surrounding this difficult occurrence. Treating every police shooting as a response to risk, threat and danger is mandatory, yet there is something unsettling about having to kill someone as it fulfilled some desire on their part. It certainly is a selfish act, as it did not take the officer's feelings and long-term implications into account and it may well leave long-term residue that diminishes the officers' psychological well-being.

Determining who the police should partner with and call upon, if and when a similar situation occurs in the future, is of critical importance. Collaboration in understanding, planning, training and response is a wise and competent approach to this response issue, and well as others. Police and other first responders, in combination with mental health, substance abuse and other providers, reduce the complexity of situational problems.

Police have a broad array of duties and obligations that include law enforcement, peace-keeping, problem solving and other domestic duties. Yet, within this uniqueness, there are similarities of purpose with other provider agencies. Thus, training for unusual events, in conjunction with other agencies (such as Crisis Intervention Training), elevates options to determine solutions and increase positive outcomes. Given that many agencies share the same client, but that this information is not generally known due to privacy rules, it would seem appropriate to determine an "early warning system" that would allow limited access and also elevate engagement where appropriate.

Example Where Systems Fail

The original call for service reported a residential disturbance. The Officer arrived and determined that a highly excited individual, with known mental health issues, was agitated. The situation was calmed to a tolerable dimension, and with family involvement, a call was placed to the Crisis Intervention Program. There was one person on duty taking calls, who stated, "*If warranted, an on-call person could be summoned, but the time frame was several hours*".

The officer was summoned back to the residence as the situation was again chaotic. Confrontation resulted and spilled out onto a public street. A second officer was dispatched and on arrival at the scene, the suspect immediately charged the officer who was exiting from the cruiser, pinning him against the cruiser, yelling, biting, and trying to grab the officer's weapon. The level of violence, the individual's level of aggravation, and the danger of serious injury, resulted in the second officer's rapid assessment that included the potential need for deadly force. Following a protracted battle, the individual was taken into custody.

A post-event concern by the second officer was the thought that deadly force was contemplated, as he was in jeopardy of severe harm. The agitated individual seemed oblivious to pain. It was unsettling, as was the realization of the quickness of a situation reaching a high level of danger.

Another concern, several vehicles stopped during the fracas and not only did no one exit to help; no calls were placed to 911 reporting an officer in an allocation. This was disturbing, and should be, for the public seemed to have taken the position that it had nothing to do with them. Difficult to explain.

In closing, it seems critically important to create a standing collaboration among responders who work with all manner of social issues and problems. Bringing together the variety of disciplines and knowledge to address community needs is common sense. Prevention is more cost effective, reduces harm, and leads to early intervention and sustainable solutions. We need to change the response model to one whose emphasis lies in prevention, education and diversity of response. No single agency has the resources or expertise to be the sole provider of complex and diverse needs in society. Does it not make sense that in combination with other expertise and experience that we can improve services and sustainable outcomes? I think it does!

Strategies Accompanying Intent: (by book authors)

1. When the initial call comes into the 911 Center, it is incumbent that dispatch personnel are trained to ask important questions and provide that information to the responding officers.

 A. A template of questions to be asked is important to insure that the full extent of information is obtained.

 B. Information obtained must be transmitted to responding officers as the more that is known, the greater the options for resolution.

Chapter 6
Rejecting Tradition – Seeking and Offering Help:
The Role of Emotional Intelligence

I. Understanding & Strengthening Emotional Intelligence

The very use of the word "emotion" can trigger a negative reaction in the strongest of men and women. Yet, our emotions are one of the baseline operating systems we possess and in dangerous situations they provide the adrenalin to react appropriately. Centuries ago, when our ancestors were beginning to walk upright, they survived, or not, using their basic emotions as autonomic responses to danger. The more common terms are **"fight or flight"** and refer to the ability to sense and react to danger, This was not a rational process where critical thinking occurred, it was more non-rational, gut level reaction that demanded mind and body action.

We know that emotions are a routine part of our daily lives. While we are not always conscious of them, they keep us balanced in a fast paced world. Situations change moment by moment as new sensory information is received and processed. Encounters vary; depending on the environment and one's role, there may or may not be time or ability to adjust accordingly.   The question is, what do we allow others to see and what do we keep below the surface, and why?

What does happen, by choice or not, is that we react to our environment with physiological, psychological and emotional responses. Our actions may mirror this reaction or it may not, depending on our ability to maintain control. Internally, the effects of stress, adversity and trauma do occur and, over time, can be harmful to our health. We are, however, capable of learning strategies and techniques that help manage to better control our emotion.

Table 4.1

Partial list of emotions

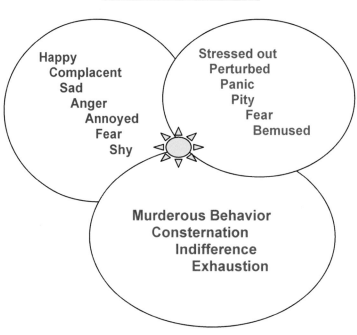

Happy
Complacent
Sad
Anger
Annoyed
Fear
Shy

Stressed out
Perturbed
Panic
Pity
Fear
Bemused

Murderous Behavior
Consternation
Indifference
Exhaustion

Different types of emotion represent "potential" responses given a particular situation or circumstance. We seldom consider how we get through the day; managing ourselves and knowing that some of what we are feeling cannot be displayed or allowed out of the privacy of our mind. For the most part, we do not like to display our emotions (or do we?) when others are around. This is especially true for people who work in and with the public. Anger is one of the more prominent emotions, that we express, more so than any other. For greater understanding we will look at emotions and their source within our physical and psychological centers, what happens in response to events, and how we can harness them for our benefit.

We now shift gears and look at the influence and impact of understanding how emotional intelligence, managing yourself and others, is a critical component to success in every area of human activity. That includes personal and professional life as well as with family, friends, colleagues, and other person to person engagement.

Example:

Joan was promoted to a supervisory position last week, one of five new supervisors. She has twelve years as a Correctional Officer, an excellent work record, attended training that was of benefit to her skills in performing her job, has maintained a positive attitude and enjoys working with people.

On Monday she reported to work in her new role and with new responsibilities prominently part of her thinking. She met with her supervisor to obtain instructions and familiarize herself with the expectations of her boss. He seems upset and says,

> "*Bob Smith has messed-up again and I want you to fix this problem!*" He shoves a stack of papers at her and says, "*I met with him just two weeks ago and told him he needed to shape up! His problem is lateness and we cannot keep spending overtime money to cover his job, I want it stopped! We can meet later to talk about my expectations.*"
>
> She takes Bob Smith's folder and heads for her office.
>
> Questions:
>
> What emotional feeling is Joan likely to be experiencing at this moment?
>
> 1. _____
>
> 2. _____
>
> 3. _____

What is Emotional Intelligence?

A brief overview of emotional intelligence and the body's system and reaction to danger and other emotional triggers will help put the concept and applications into perspective.

1. Origins of feelings:

In our early human stages of development, we were mostly reactionary in response to basic survival needs. A tiny walnut sized part of the brain is the center of nonverbal sensory input that warns of danger, reads the environment, and responds by sending impulses to the brain where functions are triggered. This small but important section of the brain, known as the **Amygdala** (uh-mig'-dull-uh), has three primary functions:

A. This almond-shaped neuro structure is involved in producing and responding to nonverbal signs of **anger, avoidance, defensiveness**, and **fear**.

B. The amygdala inspires aversive cues, such as the **freeze reaction, sweaty palms**, and the **tense-mouth display**.

C. The amygdala is a primeval *arousal center*, originating in early fishes, which is central to the expression of <u>negative emotions</u> in man.

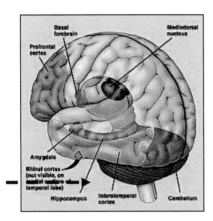

As police officers, corrections, fire, EMT and other emergency responders know, exposure to danger or unusual circumstance triggers your ability to "sense" that all is not right and you automatically begin to respond to these feelings, some of which are not yet consciously being considered. This "sense" or array of feelings emerges from the amygdala.

All thoughts other than the immediate concern, sense of danger or of routine and random thoughts, go away and your ability to focus and process information immediately in front of you becomes very keen.

Example.

A fire fighter enters a burning building processing all manner of observations, signals and sounds, seeking potential danger that experience says may be deadly. To the casual observer, entering a burning building at all is considered very dangerous, but to a trained and experienced fire fighter, there is safety awareness and conscious feeling that something has or is changing.

We respond to these sensory signals in a variety of ways. These gestures often reflect the amygdala's ongoing turmoil. For example, in an anxious meeting, we may unconsciously *flex our arms*, *lean away*, or *angle away* from a colleague who is upset. Lip, neck, and shoulder muscles may *tense* as the amygdala activates brain–stem circuits designed to produce protective facial expressions (see, e.g., <u>tense–mouth</u>)).

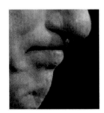

We may take a protective postures (e.g., crouch) when danger is close or feelings of extreme threat are coursing through us. The amygdala will prompt releases of adrenaline and other hormones into the blood stream, stepping–up an *avoider's response* and disrupting the control of rational thought. We "react" and the body takes a natural move toward protection. A loud bang near a crowd of people will cause many to duck down, and depending on the proximity and loudness some will fall to the ground instinctively. There is momentary confusion, some people scream reflexively, others experience the inability to react immediately and still another automatically begins to run or flee from perceived danger, not yet clarified.

Pre-avoidance system activation occurs when the senses detect protection is needed. For example, standing in front of an intoxicated and argumentative person a police officer instinctively presents a side profile. This is to protect face, chest, stomach, groin and knees from a frontal attack - areas where we are most vulnerable. Training and past experience enhance this early warning triggering response. Our rational thinking and conscious processing aspect of who we are goes "out the window" when we confront extreme danger or a situation that triggers an emotional response of some type. It is automatic in most instances and does not wait for your brain to process consciously such things as "what - if", "if this - then that action" - it is more reflexive and you automatically prepare for action. Our emotional control center and home to our personality is located in the brain's frontal lobes. This area of our brain is involved in the following activities:

1. Motor function   (raising arms, walking, bending, etc.)
2. Problem solving   (reasoning and considering what we know)
3. Spontaneity   (those unanticipated actions - laughter)
4. Memory   (recall and associations)
5. Language   (speak one or more languages)
6. Initiation   ("hey john, want to go for lunch?")
7. Judgment   (right from wrong, take action or not)
8. Impulse control   (refrain from angry outburst)
9. Social   (interaction with people, attending)
10. Sexual behavior.   (that opens a lot of behavior doors)

If we damage the area of our brain that contains the frontal lobe, we may have difficulty interpreting environmental input of information that offers feedback from the situation we find ourselves in. The effect might be difficulty in making comparison with previous experience and learning to respond to the current situation with high probability of success, a shading of learned rules that may lead to unnecessary risk-taking where you stubbornly or tenaciously persist when the danger is too high.

If a public safety officer is injured and it involves head trauma, thorough medical examination and testing is required, or should be. We can sometimes enter into a situation where the normal cautions learned from training or experience is lessened and our exposure to danger is elevated. Additionally, frontal lobe damage can be dramatic in personality changes. No assumptions should be taken; strong medical examination is the key determinant of unreasonable behavior that is post injury influenced.

Ok, why is this information important? We must understand that who we are is a simple combination of family, education and/or religious upbringing. Emotions react with situations we find ourselves in where some response is solicited. While automatic responses do take place, there may be some doubt or hesitation that can result in choice of action questioning. We do mitigate uncertainty and resulting action through training and reinforcement that experience allows.

Examples:

- A near traffic accident on the way to work leaves one's emotions in several states (depending on your degree of contribution to the event or not).

- Walking into your office and encountering an employee who is complaining about something you find of no issue (*"ok, God, not this idiot again"*!) - may trigger a response that in calmer times would not find its way to your appearance (facial expression, body posture, eye expression, fists clenched, etc.).

- Encountering a citizen in a high state of anguish whose response is anger or refusal to comply to an officer's request, may escalate unless the officer takes steps to assess and react appropriately. This is time limited, but often we react to anger with anger and it may not be the most appropriate response.

Personal Exercise:

Consider someone you know who encountered a situation that was out of the norm. What was that situation and what were the reactions that took place? Be specific in your description. We want to get at the emotions involved.

We examined emotions as they emerge from our brain within the context of situation and event. Human development continues to evolve and sophistication in behavior due to social influence, training, or other influences has helped growth and development. However, some of our basic emotional responses, for example "fight or flight," are ingrained in our automatic response to danger and threat to our emotional and physical well-being.

For example, you are walking along a downtown street and suddenly observe two people emerge from a bank, faces covered with masks, a gun in their hands, and a shot is fired. With limited information, the suddenness of the event, the lack of more information, a myriad of thoughts and emotions rush to the forefront. Reaction is going to be varied by all of those who witness the same event in the same proximity. Each of our reactions will be somewhat similar and again, with a degree of variance based on experience and other factors.

Training and experience provide responses to situations we consider threatening or dangerous. Still, for those whose lives are not accustomed to traumatic events, response can range from being unable to move to fleeing away from the perceived danger. Gathering information, observing what the cause of the initial fright was and processing the information to discern if one is in continuing danger, takes place rapidly. The scene may seem to be unfolding in slow motion or because of some familiarity the picture of what is happening forms quickly. In any case, reaction will occur and modify as time moves forward, hopefully quick enough to minimize the exposure to a dangerous situation.

If you stop and take stock of a moment in your life (not while driving you automobile or other situation where conscious awareness is important) to do the following, you may be surprised by the outcomes.

Each of us is bombarded with all manner of sensory input. This includes what we see, hear, smell, touch, taste and encounter (such as stumbling on a tree root while walking in the woods). Awareness is limited, how could it not be? We see straight ahead and with limited side vision. Hearing can be impaired, diminishing sounds. Human ability to smell, touch and taste and differentiate things is also limited when compared with other animals.

People view the world in frames, taking in that which is facing us, but with limited sensory input by those things behind and out of vision. Imagine the variety of inter-related events that are happening around us at the same moment? What is it that catches our mind and allows us to consider them? What of the larger 'moving parts' we cannot see but may sense, and which could impact on us at any moment? Who and what we are. When something happens that catches our attention, we focus more closely, narrowing the mind to gather more input on what we are concentrating on. In other words, we have a unique sense of focus that allows decision making and corresponding action

In the world of police and first responders, anticipation and caution are often accompanying conditions while on and off-duty. If awareness is heightened for long periods of time, it has an effect. We go from slow to fast instantaneously, and the body responds in like manner. Is there a cost over time, is health endangered, are our emotions and stress levels harmed over time? Based on all evidence, yes!

2. Understanding Emotional Intelligence:

Research and the application of emotional intelligence (EI) to decision-making, behavior and performance have shown to be extremely positive to the individual and to those they associate with. Emotional intelligence allows a person to recognize his or her own feelings and those of other people. This skill allows us to motivate others and to manage emotions in ourselves and with other people that we engage with.

The very use of the word "*emotion*" can trigger a negative reaction in the strongest of men. Yet, our emotions are one of the baseline operating systems we possess and in dangerous situations, for example, provide the adrenalin to react appropriately.

Stein and Book[49] provide the following indicators of EI.

- A set of skills that enables us to make our way in a complex world.

- The personal, social and survival aspects of overall intelligence, the elusive common sense and sensitivity that are essential to effective daily functioning.

- Street smarts and common sense.

> Emotional Intelligence is a learned capability and helps guide personal performance.

- The ability to read the political and social environment, and landscape them; to intuitively grasp what others want and need, what their strengths and weaknesses are; to remain unruffled by stress; and to be engaging, the kind of person that others want to be around.

- The capacity for recognizing our own feelings and those of others, for motivating ourselves, and for managing emotions in ourselves and in our relationships. It describes abilities distinct from, but complimentary to, academic intelligence, the cognitive capacities measured by IQ.

Emotional intelligence is defined as the capacity for recognizing our own feelings and in others, to motivate and manage emotions that guide thought and action. It helps to understand the difference between one's mind (reasoning, cognitive processes) and heart (emotions). When in dangerous situations, we need to remain calm and to consider alternatives, safety procedures and other cognitive processes.

Emotional intelligence is a learned capability and helps guide performance. It is also a critical component central to leadership and helping others do their job more effectively. A good leader is able to tune into how others are feeling and thinking, to read the impact of a decision or action required of others and to respond accordingly.

The U.S. Navy[50] utilizes emotional intelligence training to improve leadership and personal command style. Some of the outcomes of that research found that superior leaders:

> - Balanced a people oriented personal style with a decisive command role,
> - Did not hesitate to take charge, be purposeful, assertive, and businesslike,
> - Were more positive and outgoing,
> - Were more emotionally expressive and dramatic,
> - Were warmer and more sociable (smile, friendlier, democratic, cooperative, fun to be with), appreciative and trustful,

---

[49] . Stein, S. & Book, H. (2000). The EQ Edge. Toronto, Canada. Stoddart Pub.

[50] Knowing: Self as an Agent of Change.
http://www.au.af.mil/au/awc/awcgate/navy/knowing/knowing_selfaschange.htm

> Task oriented and firm in expectations.

Mediocre Leaders displayed the following traits:

> Harsh
> Negative
> Legalistic
> Egocentric
> Taskmaster
> Disapproving
> Tough-minded
> Led by the book
> More domineering
> Aloof and self-centered
> More authoritarian and controlling
> Legalistic and inflexible standards (e.g., Movie "Mr. Roberts").

According to the Emotional Intelligence model, there are five components[51]. They are:

1. Knowing one's emotions,
2. Managing emotions,
3. Motivating oneself,
4. Recognizing emotions in others, and
5. Handling relationships.

The first three are categorized as competencies which determine how we manage ourselves, while the last two are those which determine how we handle relationships. Under the first component of EI, - knowing one's emotions – we are focusing on a true self-awareness, or recognizing a feeling as it happens. A greater sense of self-awareness provides the ability to make more realistic assessments or our own capabilities and self-confidence, which channels us to better decision making.

PERSONAL COMPETENCE DOMAINS[52]

I. Self-Awareness
II. Self-Regulation
III. Motivation
IV. Empathy
V. Social Skills

I. Self-Awareness Domain	
Knowing one's internal states, preferences, resources, and intuitions	
1. Emotional awareness.	Recognizing one's emotions and their effects.
2. Accurate self-assessment	Knowing one's strengths and limits.
3. Self-confidence	A strong sense of one's self-worth and

---

[51]. Rosene, R. (2005:14). Naval Leadership Assessment & Development. U.S. Army War College.
[52]. Goleman, D. (1998). Working with Emotional Intelligence. New York, NY. Bantam Books.

	capabilities

❖

II. Self-Regulation Domain	
Managing one's internal states, impulses, and resources	
1. Self-Control	Keeping disruptive emotions and impulses in check
2. Trustworthiness	Maintaining standards of honesty and integrity
3. Conscientiousness	Taking responsibility for personal performance
4. Adaptability	Flexibility in handling change
5. Innovation	Being comfortable with novel ideas, approaches, and new information

❖

III. Motivation Domain	
Emotional tendencies that guide or facilitate reaching goals	
1. Achievement Drive	Striving to improve or meet a standard of excellence
2. Commitment	Aligning with the goals of the group or organization
3. Initiative	Readiness to act on opportunities
4. Optimism	Persistence in pursuing goals despite obstacles and setbacks

❖

IV. Empathy Domain	
Awareness of others' feelings, needs, and concerns	
1. Understanding Others	Sensing others' feelings and perspectives, and taking an active interest in their concerns
2. Developing Others	Sensing others' developmental needs and bolstering their abilities
3. Service Orientation	Anticipating, recognizing, and meeting customers' needs
4. Leveraging Diversity	Cultivating opportunities through different kinds of People
5. Political Awareness	Reading a group's emotional currents and power relationships

❖

V. Social Skills Domain	
Adeptness at inducing desirable responses in others	
1. Influence	Wielding effective tactics for persuasion
2. Communication	Listening openly and sending convincing messages

3. Conflict Management	Negotiating and resolving disagreements
4. Leadership	Inspiring and guiding individuals and groups
5. Change Catalyst	Initiating or managing change
6. Building Bonds	Nurturing instrumental relationships
7. Collaboration & Cooperation	Working with others toward shared goals
8. Team Capabilities	Creating group synergy in pursuing collective goals

Emotional intelligence has been described as "an array of non-cognitive capabilities, competencies and skills that influence one's ability to succeed in coping with environmental demands and pressures" (**Reuven Bar-On**[53]). It can be illustrated by the following descriptors:

- Set of skills that allows you to make your way in a complex world
- Personal, social and survival aspects of overall intelligence
- Common sense
- Sensitivity essential to effective daily functioning (street smarts)
- Ability to read the political and social environment
- Intuitively grasp what others want and need
- Read other peoples strengths and weaknesses
- Remain unruffled by stress
- To be engaging (the kind of person others want to be around)

3. Applying emotional intelligence to assisting citizens and communities organize and prepare for man-made or nature disasters.

The following case study provides an example of an event that occurs and how different emotions are involved. Read the study and respond to the questions that follow.

Case Study

You have been summoned to the Mayor's office to discuss your next year's budget. The Mayor greets you warmly, as is her usual manner, offers you coffee and invites you to make yourself comfortable.

She says, *"As you are aware, the Council will begin discussion on the city's budget next week. They made it clear that each city department must cut a minimum of 10 percent from their overall budget and asked me to meet with each department head to convey that message. I know it will be difficult and I hate to spring this on you at this late hour, but I need your cooperation and assistance to get this done!"*

---

[53] . Bar-On, R. (2002). *EQ-I: Bar-On emotional quotient inventory technical manual.* Toronto, Canada: Multi-Health Systems.

At this point your naturally tendency is to argue with the Mayor, pointing out that the department's budget is mostly personnel wages and fringe benefits. You want to ask where in God's name are you going to find that kind of cut, but to do so at this point is only reactionary and not with supporting data. You determine that you will go back to your office, call in the person who knows most about the budget, discuss options, and plan a strategy.

That is not a new scenario to most readers and the question is what aspects of your emotions are being affected by the situation as read? Is it purely a cognitive (thinking) problem or are other aspects of who you are being called into play? It is important to consider similar life experiences and determine how you reacted and what might have been different in hindsight.

What this means when working within your community.

1. Know and understand yourself first. What makes you do what you do and what is the rationale behind these motivations? You can be clear on helping others when you are able to articulate clearly the values and goals you set for yourself and when asking others to help.

2. When you reach out to a community, you are asking people to buy-in and to believe in your vision and reasons for the request. This requires your being able to appeal to their needs, to see ahead into a future that is not present and where some of the ideas being presented might not be within their grasp. You become a salesman.

3. Respect for other opinions and ideas. When we engage people we must be willing and able to understand their thoughts, blend them with ours and seek a common and workable forward motion. With agreement comes increased motivation and commitment. Building community capacity to prepare for natural and man-made disasters or other emergency situations is partially on faith and partially on solid planning. Working with others requires engagement in both arenas.

4. Social skills, talking, listening, resolving issues, identifying and solving problems as well as other mutual understanding is not always easy. We must be willing to engage from an honest position and work with others, accommodating their needs and ideas as well. This will, in time, result in achievement of the established goals.

5. Collaborate with others. Who else should be present to offer expertise, ideas, resources and willing participation? We recommend starting with existing services, those individuals in the community with expertise, training and established roles. This list includes Fire, Police, EMS, Emergency Management and others at local, county, state and federal agencies. It is also important to identify people with expertise in the community who will offer this knowledge to the working group. This includes all manner of people including medical, energy, construction, life sustaining services, and others who will be identified.

Summary:

  With police and other first responders, mention of the word emotion is tantamount to slamming a door shut. Everyone knows that emotions equate to being soft or to immediately refrain from further discussion. There is the belief one must be tough, not let things bother you, to tell someone to "suck it up" and move forward.

  Yet, within the human body are multiple systems that are autonomic in response, outside of our control and that often becomes triggered in specific situations. Ignored, there is an accumulation of stress, which by itself is required in moderation, but too much, over a period of years, can turn deadly.

  In this chapter we seek to understand as to why we sometimes feel like we do. But more importantly, by knowing this, what can we do to minimize harmful effects from long-term exposure to negative, dangerous, and stressful events? Repeating a statement from the beginning of this chapter:

  We know that emotions are a routine part of our daily lives and while we are not always conscious of them, they keep us balanced in a fast paced world. Situations change moment by moment as new sensory information is received and is processed. Encounters vary and depending on the environment and one's role, there may or may not be time or proclivity to adjust timely. The key is, what do we allow others to see and what do we keep below the surface, and why.

For the value it carries, pretending that years of encounter with stressful events, deviance, death and destruction and other emotional situations, traumatic to health and well-being is not harmful, is to follow the advice that burying one's head in the sand, as it equates to all will be well! We can bring balance to the lives of people who work in high stress occupations, with a subtle mindset change.

Chapter 7
Strategies to Build and Shape Personal Resilience

Introduction

     We take exceptional care to outfit our police and first responder officers with all manner of equipment and tools to protect their physical well-being. We do not provide skills and tools that are equally powerful in protecting the psychological and emotional well-being of our personnel. More must be done due to the culture and isolation that eventually takes place among police and first responders officers (Police, Fire, EMS, Corrections, others). Resilience training assists in addressing this issue in a planned and thorough manner.

     Concern with the plight of police officers, fire fighters, EMTs and other public safety personnel as they engage in their career, serves not only as a path to retirement benefits, it also diminishes life, attitude, humor, and leaves a life style of ill health and skewed mental reservations. A trail of sadness involving family matters, financial struggles, and personal disarray, often results. One acquires a deviated societal outlook that considers people as corrupt, a world filled with idiots and criminals and no one is to be trusted other than those who have traveled the same path, other police and first responders'.

Stone (2013)[54] emphasized the importance of addressing the effects of frequent encounters with traumatic events. A single life-time experience is enough for most people, a twenty-five year job related exposure leaves scars and sleep interruption and unless this is addressed, harm to the individual is the outcome. Stone cited that as many as 37 percent of firefighters can be diagnosed with PTSD symptoms. His illustration that following the school shooting mayhem in Newtown, Connecticut, more than 16 percent of the 43-member police force took leave for PTSD issues. And, make no mistake, it does not gradually fade and then all is well. It lingers, burrows deeper into one's psyche and manifests itself in ways most people cannot conceive.

A career spent working society's problems, investigating violence, providing care and custody to people who victimized other humans, an observer of what the worst in society offers, corrodes the officer's sense of right from wrong, well-being from predator, and a disintegrating belief in the good of man. The journey takes its toll, one day at a time, and as the years pass by the once robust and healthy officer is burdened with numerous negative physical and mental deficits that have eroded his life and those of family far quicker than other careers.

     This need not be the case, as the well-being of employees should be a primary concern of the organization. Providing the tools that offer safety over harm, we freely give firearms, handcuffs, Taser weapons, pepper spray, bullet proof vest and baton in support of officer safety. Yet the officers mental health and attitudes that maintain a balance in life, are often totally neglected and non-existent. There are programs

---

[54] Stone, A. (2013, Sept/Oct). *Beyond Debriefing*. Emergency Management magazine. E. Republic

available to the organization and its administrative and supervisor staff that can substantially reduce the effects of years of dealing with society's negativity, brutality and violence.

The Path to Dysfunction

Responding to citizen calls for assistance, managing inmates in a large prison facility, or responding to a fire where danger shadows every action, eventually leads to the accumulation of negative stress related residue, which, over time, results in negative emotions, anger, impatience and unsettling feelings. Change in personality and behavior is subtle but change nonetheless occurs. Duties associated with doing one's job may lead to confrontation with an armed and dangerous person and in the ensuing fight, justifiably kills that individual. Officers have been killed in the line of duty resulting in tragic outcomes and substantially affecting the emotions and attitudes of the survivors. Other maladies can be serious and impact the officer and family, they include depression, use of substances (both alcohol and drugs), heightened high risk lifestyle, eroding and more negative attitude problems, relationship problems, and all manner of aberrant and deviant behavior. Additionally, safety officers have higher mortality rates for cancer and heart disease than the general public, with stress thought to be a major contributor.

These issues certainly extend into family life with higher than average divorce rates than the general public. Officers often suffer in their intimate relationships and often do not fulfill the normal role of parent with their children. The extent of this internal trauma is reflected by the statistic that the average U.S. suicide rate is 12 per 100,000. A study by the Fraternal Order of Police showed police at 22 per 100,000 officer members, a truly frightening fact (Gilmartin, 2002[55]). Statistics on officer suicide differ given the study being done, the population size, and the accuracy of reports when investigation takes place.

Suffering is not lost on the individual officer, as it also impacts family, friends, colleagues, and others. The officer's attention diverts and family and non-police friends move to a secondary place in a world that is viewed with increasing suspicion. Negativity leads to anger that often manifests when encountering tense situations or when the officer confronts challenge to his or her authority. Anger is frequently directed at the department's administration and a polarity exists that creates a division among people who are supposed to be doing the same job and on the same team. Even among colleagues, some officers are drawn to particular individuals creating a sub-culture within a sub-culture, generating suspicion and barriers where inter-personal communications are minimal. Police departments do not generally put high value on officer mental health and attitude, addressing behavior problems only when the shoe drops and someone has complained. Prevention is not yet the preferred response within police and first responder organizations.

The type of dysfunction is only limited by imagination as it manifests itself in numerous ways. And perhaps the most disheartening of all indicators is the officer's unwillingness to seek help through counseling or therapy, preferring to live with the

---

[55] Gilmartin, K. (2002). Emotional Survival for Law Enforcement. E-S Press.

trauma and sliding down the slippery slope of poor and declining physical and mental health.

Case Example

John could not sleep, he had been awake for over 48 hours working a drug case that resulted in many arrests and included serious resistance by those arrested. Shots had been fired and one suspect was injured resulting in hours of talking with Internal Affairs and writing reports. He was angry that the department acted as if the officers had done something wrong and he considered them pencil pushers who needed to get a life. When the guys were finally cut loose they went to a cops bar and had a couple of beers to unwind and discuss why they even bothered anymore.

John arrived home tired, hungry and a little hung over to find his wife had been up waiting for him and not hearing anything had called his supervisor to see if he was alright. That led to a fight over her minding her business and a statement to "*leave me alone for I've had enough crap for one day*." She took their son and left to visit with her sister, saying "*she needed to be with someone sane for a while.*"

Frustrated and angry over the earlier events and the argument with his wife, the one person who should understand, he opened yet another beer and brooded over how his life has gone from bad to worse, questioning the very fabric of his role as a police officer. A job he once cherished and felt that he could make positive change in the lives of innocent people, was in the pits and all justice was gone. As time went by; he became more cynical and withdrawn, preferring the company of the guys he worked with and classifying all others as assholes. He was not sleeping well, did not eat balanced meals, smoked and drank far too much alcohol. His marriage was in jeopardy and lately he was short of breath when exertion was required. He was overweight and looked at the world as a lost cause, even the police department brass were corrupt and did not give a shit about anything except their own welfare. If it were not for street cops like him, the whole city would be run by criminals. He recounted that in the last year he and his guys had come across tens of thousands of dollars in cash lying around and could have helped themselves, but didn't. He now questioned whether or not he would be so honest in the future. If no one gives a shit, why should he?

The Sub-Culture Path

John's story is repeated across this country a hundred times daily as Police, Corrections, Fire, EMS and other safety officers encounter situations that elicit anger and despair over a system that seems in disarray and at times to be the enemy of working officers. Police and first responders provide critical services to their communities. Their ability to cope with stressful situations and catastrophe is co-dependent on overcoming personal problems and emerging without lasting negative effects (e.g., stress, physical & mental health issues, alcohol & substance abuse, divorce, increase in liability & torts, etc.). As the officer's world view narrows and he or she becomes more cynical and distanced from normality, desperateness enters his/her thinking and filters what is seen and heard, bending reality into a view that may become, and often is, jaded.

The accumulation of negative experience and stressful encounters has a negative impact on an individual that, left untreated, may be disastrous. Over time the job becomes all consuming, distorts the officers thinking and intensifies the need to be engaged with peers and engaged in exciting situations.

Police and first responders provide a variety of emergency service roles, while the circumstances vary the impact on individuals is essentially the same. The results include poor performance, physical and mental health issues, damaged relationships, high divorce, suicide and other traumatic events are all too common. A variety of psychological, physiological, and behavioral manifestations arise, increasing individual overreaction and error. When the person experiencing these symptoms is a police or other first responder, it is of major concern given their role and responsibilities to the larger society.

It is considered demeaning to directly address these issues with a dysfunctional employee. But, can we continue to ignore the symptoms and signals of an individual employee under distress, waiting until he or she self-destructs and all manner of care and consideration evaporate as issues of liability emerge and the employee is put on disciplinary notice?

Coping with stress and dysfunction that extends into personal, family, social and work life often assumes abnormal proportions that left unaddressed, lead toward destruction. Supervisory staff will seek to "straighten out" the individual using threat and punishment, peers in some cases, reinforce the negative attitudes, while others choose to give up and walk away, unable to tolerate further abuse. If the problems were not so widespread they could be ignored, but that is not the case. Without proper training support and organizational commitment to overcome dysfunction, it rarely repairs itself.

What is Resilience and Why All the Hype?

Resilience is the power to adapt well to adversity and to cope with stress, grief, concern, worry, tragedy and crisis in your life. It means you can get back to a sense of normalcy and feelings of well-being. You regain control of your life as it relates to family, friends, work, and other commitments you make. It means that those significant others in your life regain their sense balance as you are not posing a threat or creating trauma due to your personal dysfunction.

> Resilience is the power to adapt well to adversity and to cope with stress, grief, concern, worry, tragedy and crisis in your life.

of

Strengthening personal resilience is one of the primary focus areas providing skills to help manage crisis, reduce everyday stressful situations, and being more effective in meeting job and personal demands that are associated with everyday living. The rationale is simple; there are too many people suffering from a myriad of problems and issues that include: stress, heart problems, poor diet, obesity, respiratory / smoking, alcohol and substance abuse, divorce and other issues. With relationship to work and other organizations, considerable work time is lost due to illness or stress related issues that end up costing greatly in overtime to replace. And, poor performance, disciplinary issues, and occasionally liability situations arise due to employee distraction from work duties. Like an accumulation of dust on a window sill, the residue referenced here is not beneficial to the individual's physical or mental health. Some events are so traumatic that the impact on thinking and behavior, from that moment forward changes the person, not always in a positive manner.

Four Considerations of Endurance and Resilience.

1. Endurance and resilience skills and attitudes are key factors in wellness and health maintenance programs. Resilience skills like flexibility and problem solving help an individual and the organization cope with adversity while continuing to provide critical services. Resilience skills are offered in many venues and the program assists organizations and employees to manage stress, promote wellness, accepting change, and help build team spirit and increase job satisfaction.

2. Endurance and resilience provides tools that help individuals and organizations overcome unusual and traumatic situations that, when encountered, are difficult to reconcile and resolve. Any number of events can combine to create the need for strategies to bring balance to employees. This includes the death of a colleague, loss of funding, unusual negative events and other traumatic situation that requires assistance to be provided to employees to help them deal with stress and thus improve their overall mental and physical health and relationships with colleagues, family, and friends.

3. Endurance and resilience development is personally helpful. When trouble strikes, it is difficult to distract thinking from the overwhelming problems and simultaneously make appropriate decisions and execute actions that ease the burden and bring resolution. Providing and refocusing effective skills and attitudes is the primary outcome of resilience training. Training helps identify ways to manage personal and peer employee needs that accompany constant exposure to high stress situations. These same tools are useful when encountering short term problems that demand immediate solutions.

4. Endurance and resilience development assists people to acquire special skills and knowledge useful in addressing personal needs and to establish balance in their life. Working with people one often encounters a variety of emotions that reflect the individual's encounter with a situation that is overwhelming and traumatic. Unless the individual learns to manage the emotions and trauma it is very difficult to learn new skills, maintain focus, establish a pathway to change, find the strength to continue on, and any number of relational needs. Resilience training helps find balance and allow continued progress toward change and a new path to success.

Strengthening Individual Resilience

The capacity of a person to learn skills that assist in resisting and overcoming debilitating events and accumulated stress is a powerful means of remaining balanced in work, family, personal, and social life involvements. Developing resilience permits a person to rise up from an overwhelming event that has caused great discomfort or peril to one's well-being or safety. Experiencing a traumatic event causes a person to feel numbness, heaviness in their chest, racing heart, shallow breathing and more. It often elicits a response resulting in dysfunction and disbelief of what just happened. Not all events are of sudden major trauma. Some gradually accumulate overtime until sufficient tension increases, resulting in unbearable stress and severe symptoms that cause increased concern.

When encountering these conditions, routine daily events become difficult to accomplish and the mind and body seek comfort through withdrawal, isolation or diversion. Escape mechanisms include the use of alcohol, drugs, over eating, and taking unusual risks with the resultant feelings of anxiety, depression and eventually burnout. Over time, attempts at relieving stressful conditions begin to erode normal family and work life, resulting in diminished performance and wounded relationships that suffer under the strain. The effects of stress lead to cardiovascular disease, heart and blood pressure problems, and a host of other symptoms unhealthy to the individual.

> *Over time, attempts at relieving stressful conditions begin to erode normal family and work life, resulting in diminished performance and wounded relationships that suffer under the strain.*

I will now focus on providing strategies to help police and first responders reduce the impact of traumatic and abnormal situations that may led to burnout. The question we will address is what to do about the accumulation of harmful exposure to traumatic and life changing events.

Thoughts and feelings and resultant body responses are closely tied and exhibit signals of what is happening within the individual's overall emotional state of being.

Feeling Experienced	Physical Signs
Anger	Hands-on-hips posture, pounding heart, sweating and rapid breathing, and eyes flared open, tight set of the mouth, some flushing. Directed attention to a person or others.
Rage / Fury	Clenched fists, cold focused stare, loud and rapid speech, not listening well, oblivious of surrounding. Focused on a target of the rage, seeks revenge and to harm.
Depression / Despair / Despondency	Fatigue, weighed-down posture, slouching, staring into space, a slow and hesitant voice and frequent sighing. Does not perform even small tasks well, distracted and seemingly uncaring.
Anxiety	Restlessness, pounding heart, rapid breathing, nervous energy, unable to sit still, eyes look around rapidly, and a look of tension on face. Increase worry that in turn increases anxiety.

Fear / Panic	Aching muscles and headaches, tension in next and shoulders, seemingly over-aware keeps cautious look around oneself. Desire to blindly flee if fear becomes overwhelming. Symptoms that mimic a heart attack.

Highly resilient people experience fewer physical and mental side effects of stress and are able to perform within normal limits. When a person has high resilient capability, they are able to maintain better health and well-being and generally do not experience a deep level of fatigue. In the workplace, these differences make a substantial difference in productivity versus diminished work output. The American Institute of Stress[56] estimated it costs employers $300 billion annually for stress related illness. It seems reasonable that it would cost far less to assist employees in learning resilience skills to help them reduce the effects of stress.

In both personal and organizational perspectives it is necessary to obtain skills and knowledge that will lessen the onslaught of problems and quicken their reduction. Building resilience, being able to cope and take steps necessary to combat the effects of stress, can be learned.   The ability to cope with stress and catastrophe and acquire cumulative "protective factors" that are used in planning and reducing "risk factors" that threaten or endanger a person, organization or community's well-being and security are critical skills to acquire.

Police officers learn to drive defensively, protect their physical well-being, and survive armed conflict.   But when we mention mental health and learning about symptoms and self-care, the topic is instantly diverted. Correctional officers learn when a situation does not feel right, they have to take preventive steps, how searching for weapons prevents injury and death, and that manage prisoner behavior instantly leads to fewer out of control events. Fire fighters estimate the severity and extent of a fire, the presence of accelerants or deadly chemicals, and the building's structural integrity and make decisions that are safety focused. Yet, imbalanced and destructive behaviors lead to disability, dismissal, discipline, liability and occasionally death. Resilience training provides a path to sustainable change and is equally as important as other officer safety programs. Resilience training increases an individual's social competence, problem-solving, self-sufficiency and independence, and instills a sense of purpose and belief in a bright future.

Hierarchy Levels to Organize Personal Resiliency Skills[57]

- Personal Health and Well-being. Make this a priority in your life. Often this is not considered as the demands of the job or other interests step in front of awareness on how we are feeling or who is seeking our attention. Health care, especially mental health care, can easily erode due to shortcuts in life. Unless we are paying attention, it is all too easy to fall into that negative cycle.

---

[56]. http://www.stress.org/americas.htm

[57]. Siebert, A. (2006). Haw valuable life lessons can breed resilience. ASTD, September. Additional information added by Lumb, 2013.

- <u>Problem Confrontation & Resolution</u>. Waiting and hoping for the best, works occasionally. In many instances, it is insufficient and we must take steps to make appropriate changes and find sustainable solutions to issues that confront us. Not taking steps can and does lead to higher levels of stress. When the parameters of a problem are clear, you should map out a strategy to bring about resolution.

- When that happens, it is a relief and helps return our thinking and physical systems to balance.

- <u>Healthy Mind and Body</u>. We cannot separate one from the other and it is important to keep both in balance, to address issues, to seek and engage in activities that lead to improved well-being. One complements the other and is irreversibly tied together, necessitating that we work to maintain proper health and care. It starts within us, not from some external entity.

- <u>Engaging in Self-Guidance</u>. Waiting for things to happen is an everyday, natural occurrence. The sheer volume of events and actions that surround us, take our attention and demands our engagement. Take time to list issues and needs, tasks to accomplish, items that require your attention and make a plan that may list time frame, other people who must be involved, and other considerations leading to resolution and completion. A build-up of multiple items needing attention is not only distracting, but stressful.

- <u>Accentuate the Positive Aspects of Life</u>. In some public safety jobs, the employee's work involves engagement with negativity and an almost endless array of issues and problems that are confronted. Over time, job dysfunction issues weigh heavily on our thinking and if not relieved, can be debilitating. Find those activities to engage in that bring happiness, joy, and fulfillment to your lives, and do them. Do not spend all waking hours engaged in work, either directly or in one's mind, find time to get away and do other things. Not always easy, but a necessity if you are to live a long and healthy life.

Life is all about change. Routine and habit are comfortable as is the blissful belief that life will not introduce any speed bumps. But it will! We know that people who work at being part of family, friends, workplace environment, volunteer and group involvement generally are stronger in coping with change. Finding balance, being able to cope and move with sudden change or situations that are evolving, allows you, as an individual, to adapt and move forward easier than someone who does not respond well to pressure and change.

Research tells us that resiliency and endurance is part of our learning system and our ability to adapt and to adjust. Improving our competencies, skills and using experience to work on issues and needs is something that we humans can learn to, do. Research also tells us that categorizing resiliency strengths, as follows, aids our existence, especially when something of a serious nature happens.

Level 1. Health and Well-being.

We often over-burden ourselves in daily life causing us to yield to stress. This causes us to believe that we are the "victim" of the organization that we work for. We do not stop to consider that perhaps we are contributing to our own personal discomfort. Transferring blame to someone else does not change anything, and we remain stressed. When we train ourselves to be more enduring and resilient, life changes as we grow stronger and become less prone to the effects of work and other influences.

Siebert (2006[58]), says that what most people call stress are really their internal, physical feelings of anxiety or strain they are uncomfortable with. Awareness of how we manage stress is important in bringing external forces under control, managing that which we deem harmful to our well-being. A good tool is learning how to be optimistic. We then see things more positively, begin to experience past events with less of a negative impact on ourselves. Then we find we are able to address the world from a more healthy perspective.

Level 2. Confronting Problems.

There is a connection between being able to resolve problems and our personal endurance and resiliency. Allowing a problem to rule your thinking leads to frustration and confusion that contributes to stress. It can be changed with engaged problem solving. We experience all manner of problems in life that emerge from work, relationships, fiscal, health, environment and many other influences. Productive people are problem-solvers, possess higher levels of confidence and generally are healthier. Transfer of personal well-being and happiness to external causes, is often resolved with strong self-motivated internal problem-solving. A person can control what impacts their psyche rather than allowing their mind to run amuck with all manner of conflicting emotion.

Problem solving involves taking time to clearly define the issue, list its component parts and linkages, obtain all possible information, and determine what others have used to overcome similar situations. Following the analysis of the information, selecting sustainable solutions in partnership with other stakeholders, has a better chance of success in reducing the problem at hand.

Level 3. Mind versus Body.

How we feel about ourselves (image, confidence and esteem) often dictates how we engage and do what we do as an individual. Keeping one's mind healthy is important as it allows us to expand our thinking, participate in professional development, and seek out different interests. It is not always easy to do this. At times considerable concentration and will is needed. But, at the end of the day, the gains are considerable and worth the effort.

Level 4. Self-Direction.

Enduring people are largely in control of their lives. They are good problem solvers, allow experience to help with current and future problems, are generally confident and do not see life as a negative place that leads to unhappiness. Confident people generally have a resilient personality and a sense of humor, to name a few. Confident people are resilient and often take charge during an emergency or tense

---

[58]. Siebert, A. (2006). Develop Resiliency Skills. ASTD, Sept., 88-89.

situation, when others may be paralyzed. Such is the nature of a self-directed individual.

Level 5. Accentuate the Positive.

Resiliency allows the individual to bounce back from trauma or discouraging situations and events and to use that experience to learn higher levels of response and to maintain endurance. When public safety officers, following a highly charged or negative event, engage in review of the situation, they are strengthening their planning, response, and self-management for future events.

Components of Resilience.

Resilience is the power to adapt well to adversity and to cope with stress, grief, concern, worry, tragedy and other crisis and overcome the trauma and return, in a planned way, to renewed balance in life and community functionality. It assists in returning to a sense of normalcy and feelings of well-being. Resilience promotes regaining control of your life as it relates to family, friends, work, community and other commitments you make. Resilience helps individuals and others to regain their sense of balance, productivity, and well-being as they address issues and needs relating to life challenges. Resilience training provides skills to help manage crisis, reduce everyday stressful situations, and help people to be more effective in meeting job and personal demands that are associated with everyday living.

Resilience for Police and first responders.

Resilience Training for police and first responder officials must address the needs of the organization and individuals who frequently encounter traumatic and potentially life-changing events, providing tools to help overcome negative influences. Training specifically addresses teaching police and first responders to appropriately address personal and community traumatic events in ways that lessens debilitating outcomes.

Resilience training examines the process of coping with and managing hardship and traumatic encounters that occur in the delivery of emergency services. These encounters include high danger, potential injury, unsafe situations, death, hazardous encounters, long-term exposure to violence and destruction, and a multitude of other scenarios personnel encounter. The training provides techniques to handle acute tragedy and to bounce back from difficult encounters. There are multiple benefits associated with this training.

Police, Fire, EMS, and other emergency services have an obligation to assist employees to better manage stress and thus improve their overall mental and physical health. When trouble strikes, it is difficult to distract thinking from the overwhelming problems and simultaneously make appropriate decisions and execute actions that ease the burden and brings resolution. Providing and refocusing effective skills and attitudes is the primary outcome of resilience training.

The Road to Police and First Responder Resilience Training

Our police and first responders are charged with providing specialized public services that include responsibilities of safety, rescue, custody of inmates, prevention, and other stop-gap measures that require high skill, knowledge, training, attitudes and a depth of dedication not found in everyday life. In carrying out these duties, they accumulate experiences that typically, while fulfilling, also expose them to trauma and visions of a world that can deliver devastation and harm and take away feelings of safety and well-being. The residue referenced here is not beneficial to the individual's physical or mental health. Some events are so traumatic that the impact on thinking and behavior, from that moment forward, changes the person, and not always in a positive manner.

Organizations, peers, families, friends and the individual him or herself have an option that provides a level of help that is both proactive and outcome positive. Learning to be more resilient and acquire the knowledge and skills that help maintain a healthy life-style, is positive in itself.

Police and first responders and similar agencies must address the cumulative "protective factors" that are used to keep the community safe without diminishing their individual fortitude to perform their duties. Resilience is an integral component of planning and used to oppose and reduce "risk factors" that threaten or endanger a person, an organization or a community's well-being and security. The ability to withstand enormous pressure, to react with confidence, and to effectively continue to carry out one's duties while others are incapacitated, emerges from a person's inner resilience. We also use terms to help describe resilience training as addressing the individual's hardiness, power of endurance, resoluteness, and self-assurance. This research is found in the psychological literature and our applied practice training combines theory with police and first responders practice.

Encountering significant trauma or adversity and risks associated with negative life conditions, requires the ability of the individual to adapt and overcome the situation or event that represents the threat (Luther, Cicchetti, & Becker, 2000[59]). Adverse life situations and vulnerability must be addressed to modify or prevent overwhelming negative outcomes. Resilience training and understanding the situation allows the individual, organization and community to demonstrate competence when faced with overwhelming stress and is a predictor that good outcomes can be achieved, regardless of the risk encountered. And, resilience training also develops the ability to recover from a traumatic event, to move forward and to sustain intellectual and emotional abilities thereby strengthening performance and activities (Masten, et al., 1990[60]).

The Application of Resilience Training

Resilience training has five major applications that include the following components:

1. Immediate application when handling a call for service that is fraught with heightened emotions. When others are not in control of their emotions, the officer

---

[59] Luthar, S. S., Cicchetti, D., & Becker, B. (2000). "The construct of resilience: A critical evaluation and guidelines for future work. *Child Development, 71(3)*, 543-562.

[60] Masten, A. S., Best, K. M., & Garmezy, N. (1990). Resilience and development: Contributions from the study of children who overcome adversity. Development and Psychopathology, 2, 425-444.

must be calm, observant, and aware of the environment and to respond in a manner that prevents further escalation.

2. Delayed application following an event that was traumatic or disturbed the officer triggering an emotional response. Strategies to lessen an emotional reaction are needed to maintain control over one's behavior.

3. Applied to family, friend and colleagues who experience trauma or stress.

4. Applied by a supervisor to his or her subordinates who display behavior or performance that is not within the organization's mission or policy.

5. Strategies used by the organization to maintain harmony and reduce dysfunction.

The above applications demonstrate that individuals have many skills and competencies to draw on when addressing issues or confronting problem situations. The point of importance is that we all have innate resilience capacity and when we face increased pressure, disaster, or other debilitating confrontation, we have the ability to self-right, change to meet the challenge, and implement the right course of action (Werner and Smith, 1992[61]).

Police and first responders carry primary responsibility for maintaining community security and well-being, a task in the 21st Century that is difficult at best. However, the presence of a small number of men and women trained as deputy sheriffs, police, fire, correctional officers, EMTs, medical, and other safety agency personnel cannot be the only line of defense against traumatic and potentially life-threatening events. All facets of the community, its people, businesses, social and political organizations, volunteer groups, religious and health related agencies also have an important role. The key to finding solutions to overcoming problems includes a greater level of understanding, planning and preparation, and increased ability of individuals, organizations, and communities to be resilient in the face of pending disaster and risk to life and property.

Summary Statement.

To summarize, police and first responders acquire special skills and knowledge that are useful in addressing personal needs and to establish a foundation for acquiring skills to help others to become more resilient is a primary goal of resiliency training. Public safety responders are a unique and critical service for communities and cannot be compromised due to personnel dysfunction. Addressing and reducing the effects of exposure to danger and traumatic events is a common goal of the individual employee and the organization.

---

[61] Werner, E. E., & Smith, R. S. (1992). *Overcoming the odds: High-risk children from birth to adulthood.* New York: Cornell University Press.

Key strategies to strengthen personal resilience and coping skills include.

- Establish and map out strategies to achieve goals.
- Maintain open communications with family and friends.
- Acknowledge that change is normal and that adaptation is possible.
- When confronting crisis you are confident in bringing it under control.
- Maintain a positive view of yourself and trust in your instinct and ability.
- Be decisive in your actions and address problem in a straightforward manner.
- Manage your outlook, be optimistic, and visualize where you want to be and how to get there.
- Take care of your physical and mental health managing stress and engaging in activities that you enjoy and are relaxing.

15 Strategies to Overcome Adversity, Stress, and/or Trauma[62].

The following fifteen strategies can be used to reduce the impact of stress, adversity and trauma in one's life and with those others you may elect to help. Pick and choose one or more that you find compatible with your personality and preference and learn to apply them when facing uncertainty and stress. Apply them and see how well they fit, do they offer help, if so, how can you increase your personal well-being and balance? If you have been personally involved in a situation similar to ones discussed thus far, then you know at a very deep level that you cannot simply shrug this incident off as another 'typical duty call!' Remnants of the frame by frame experience will reoccur and replay through one's mind when least expected. It must not be ignored if this is happening to you, for your personal well-being and your ability to maintain physical, mental and emotional balance in life, Is of the utmost importance.

They are applicable to both the individual and his or her supervisor.

1. Connecting with others is better than isolation.

a. Individual

- When facing demons, it is helpful to seek out a person or persons you are comfortable with and talk out this issue and seek guidance.

- Loneliness is difficult and it does not allow you the opportunity to work through issues as you tend to dwell on them, sometimes excessively.

- Being with people you know and feel comfortable with helps reduce the negativity and quickly working through problems.

---

[62] http://www.apa.org/helpcenter/road-resilience.aspx# American Psychological Association. The 15 strategies include information from the APA (reference above) and from R. Lumb, as used in other programs expanding the definition and application of each. There are additional strategies added from Lumb's list.

b. Supervisor/Organization

- If you are a <u>supervisor</u> your responsibility is to step into the breach and address performance issues. When a subordinate is not performing as expected or his or her work is affecting others the responsibility is clear. If the employee is not willing to talk with you, then explain what you are seeing, how it is affecting others, and that you are willing to, and will, assist the employee in working through the issue.

- If refusal is the response and the behavior is likely to continue, then mandatory referral to EAP or other service may be the next step. Critical point: you have a responsibility to address the issue and find resolution!

2. **Flexibility is better than rigidity.**

a. Individual

- A rigid and unyielding attitude and behavior turns people off and eventually you find yourself alone.

- Unsmiling, grim, griping and other negative behaviors are harmful to your personal health and to those who must deal with you.

- Attempt to see a broader and more open perspective. Look for the good and not only the bad or negative aspects.

- Do not seek that everything you do must be 100% perfect or else you will not participate. With an–all–or nothing attitude, you will miss out on a lot. You might find that 60% turns out well and that you are satisfied at that level of success or accomplishment.

b. Supervisor/Organization

- With frustration comes simmering anger or disquiet feelings. When a subordinate's behavior is irritating and necessitates action, it is usually at the end of a period of time when you hoped the problem would resolve itself. Guard against overreaction.

- When discussing an employee's behavior and its effect on the workplace, assuming a more open attitude to seek understanding may open the employee to a more willing partnership. When people are in a confrontation situation, it is difficult for either party to not react defensively. They tend to shut down hearing the other person, raise the level of being "on guard" and engage in other defensive mechanisms that will diminish and reduce communications.

- Start from an easy position, if possible (safety issues leave no room for negotiation) and seek the employee's compliance, asking them to weigh in on ideas to resolve the problems.

3. Communicating better than silence.

a. Individual

- Sitting alone mulling over your problems and troubles leads to deeper levels of despondency.

- Talk with people you know and respect, seek input, ask questions, find out the names of people who may be able to help.

- Telling your story helps by itself. When others weigh in and provide assistance the true benefit becomes therapeutic.

b. Supervisor/Organization

- Silence, waiting for a change or negative facial expressions of disapproval is meaningless. Meet with the employee and address the issue(s) when you have sufficient information to make your case.

- Tell the employee what you are seeing and know. Ask for their input. Seek solutions to the identified problems both from you as a supervisor and from the individual you are talking with. Their input is critical. It should not all come from you to them with your expectations only. Their buy-in can lead to successful change.

4. We can help ourselves and others solve problems.

a. Individual

- Write down the issue or problem.

- Clearly identify any variables of aspects that you feel are contributing to the issue.

- Make sure you understand the true situation and facts. Do not leave out any important Information.

- Make a "solutions chart" (see below) showing issues and problems; then list ways to overcome them. Be specific.

Solutions Chart

Issue or Problem	Potential Solutions	People that can help
Clearly state and define the component parts. Be specific. Prioritize (if it will	What are probable solutions? Be open-minded. Cross off as Steps	List names and telephone numbers of people who might be able to help or

be helpful). Provide a timeline to maintain progress.	are accomplished.	who can make a referral to someone who can.
1.	1.	1.
2.	2.	2.
3.	3.	3.

- Frequently update your chart as new information and changes begin to take place. This can become a living or tracking record of how you overcome issues and problems.

b. Supervisor/Organization

- When in the midst of an issue or problem, it is very difficult to clearly see a solution. Supervisors who seek solutions to problems involving those others who will be affected often find the results to be stronger and more sustainable. You must be willing and have skills appropriate to help someone and to engage them in the process.

- Get the employee to complete a solutions chart.

- Review with him or her and add in your suggestions and information.

- Come to agreement with the employee on a timeframe to work toward resolution.

- Conduct follow-up discussions and track progress.

5. Recognize and deal with feelings do not ignore them.

a. Individual

- Keeping your feelings tightly wrapped and insulated from other's will lead you further into your personal gloom.

- Acknowledge that you are feeling stressed, uncomfortable, edgy, and any number of other sensations. Look within if present and you will recognize you are in discomfort.

- Self-help may work or it might become necessary to talk with a professional or other service (EAP Employment Assistance Program) to get proper help. There is no shame in seeking professional assistance.

b. Supervisor/Organization

- Getting employees to discuss feelings is difficult, particularly with males and with employees of police and first responder organizations. Nonetheless, unless the discussion on what the employee is feeling is explored, there is little hope for resolution.

- If the discussion is obviously not working and your concern is deep enough, use the organization's policy to direct the employee to professional help.

6. Be self-confident and act on values, not fears.

a. Individual

- Have faith in yourself and trust your judgment.

- No shortcuts. Follow straightforward self-advice.

- Fear driven decisions are often wrong as they are made in haste and without full information that is carefully considered and weighed for accuracy.

b. Supervisor/Organization

- Most organizations have a value statement to guide employees. The unit within which a person works or his or her immediate supervisor may also have a values statement. If one exists, it should be put on the table and discussed with the troubled employee. It is prudent to do the same with the organization's mission and goals.

- See how the values coincide with the individuals values and discuss needed adjustments.

- Be sure to explain everything in clear terms, clarifying where needed.

- The goal is to give the employee confidence and to help him or her formulate a plan they can follow that is going to have positive results.

- Fear of the unknown or anticipating results that may not occur can diminish the freedom to seek solutions or to reach out to bring about appropriate change. Uncontrolled fear can paralyze the employee and stop the headlong process.

7. Find purpose and meaning in what you do.

a. Individual

- While sometimes difficult to find the motivation during times of trouble, doing something that has value to you and others that you respect and like can result in a positive pay off to you.

- Look for the positive and good outcomes in what you are doing. If it helps, make a list that states the meaning of it

102

all. Who is helped, what is the extent of that help, what can be done to make it more meaningful, etc.

- Talk with others who share the work and see what their thinking is about the value in what you and they do.

b. Supervisor/Organization

- A supervisor can help an individual explore how a job or assignment is of value and ways to find meaning.

- This is done through discussion, questions and clearly explaining and clarifying questions.

- Writing down key points and where issues of concern exist allows for later clarification and resolution of contradictory points. The goal is to eliminate barriers and difficulties to the extent possible.

- Renewing the employee's commitment and personal fulfillment in what they do is a positive outcome.

8. Engage in networking with others.

a. Individual

- This is a powerful tool. Find others who can offer help or suggestions and who may know someone or organizations that offer ideas and help to move you forward in meeting your goals and needs.

- The more people you engage with, the greater the information and options that can lead to quality outcomes.

b. Supervisor/Organization

- As a supervisor you may want to assist the employee to meet and talk with someone else who can offer insight and help. Arranging that contact is helpful.

- Follow-up to see that the meeting occurred. There is no need to inquire to the outcomes as they may be outside your need to know.

- You can continue to move the employee forward from the issue or problem to a more balanced work environment.

9. Be optimistic, not pessimistic.

a. Individual

- Look for and see the bright side and avoid the negative that is all too easy to find. When the mind jumps to a negative response or image, stop, take a minute and think consciously, "what is the good in what I am seeing or confronting?"

- Pessimism takes valuable energy from the emotions and body and diminishes creative thinking.

b. Supervisor/Organization

- It is not unusual for individuals experiencing unhappy work conditions or stress-related trauma to embrace negativity, as it helps justify already unhappy feelings.

- Supervisors, in discussion, should also point out positive aspects and to seek understanding that all is not hopeless. Look for and share program or other information that can help provide uplifting encouragement to the employee.

10. Seek professional help.

a. Individual

- When issues are greater than the individual can cope with it is important to seek professional help from someone trained and certified.

- Emotional and psychological trauma can be debilitating and harmful in many ways. Letting the symptoms persist will only worsen the condition and lead to further dysfunction.

b. Supervisor/Organization

- Supervisors must be aware of organizational policy and services that an employee can be directed to.

- When situations persist and it is clear that additional assistance is needed, the supervisor should not hesitate to direct the employee to seek that help.

- Supervisors have a responsibility to the organization and the employee and while not always popular, appropriate action is required.

11. Write about the issue/s.

a. Individual

- Writing can be therapeutic. Writing helps reduce the chaos of thinking into a more focused and linear approach to understanding what happened, where one's thinking is now and to begin the process of mapping out where you want to be.

- Writing allows the writer to sort through, to edit and revise as the story becomes clearer. Sorting out the detail is difficult when it is running in an endless loop in one's mind, causing more frustration and confusion.

- Writing is a process. To understand complexity, putting it on paper or using a word processor allows a person to make distinct categories, lump like information together, to note where relevant information is missing and to make notations or side notes where additional thinking must take place.

- Writing for oneself is private and allows total honesty of feelings, expression of anxiety, anger, and doubt – to name a few emotions. What you may hesitate to say to others can be said in private to yourself. Reliving, considering and examining again, and seeking to make sense of something, can take place as you write. You need not fear what others might think, for you are your own reviewer and critic and can best judge where you must go to bring about clarity and help with life planning.

b. Supervisor/Organization

- Many of the same principles for the individual apply to the supervisor. If a situation is conflicting or confusing, it helps to write down what is known, what remains unclear or unknown, and to make notes to help organize.

- Supervisors can also recommend that the individual, with whom he or she is assisting, write about the incident. It can be shared with the supervisor or not.

12. Tell your story to others.

a. Individual

- Telling one's story is commonplace with acts of heroism or extraordinary bravery or accomplishment. It allows others to share in the detail and it permits the story teller the opportunity to not only share but process the information as it relates to one's personality, soul, and place in the world. It may well help others in their quest to seek placement in the occupation and career.

- Story telling can be entertaining, a teaching moment, a lesson on what to do or not to do and generally beneficial to the student, of example and experience.

b. Supervisor/Organization

- Supervisors and the organization can share important information with other members of the profession using the experiences of other members. A story that is well told by the person who experienced the incident or learning outcome is believable and brings grounding of peer to peer or other employee to a stronger point of reality.

13. Use of humor.

a. Individual

- To lighten the moment is to reduce stress. When the pressure of an incident or event is oppressing, a moment of levity may shake loose the mood. We do not advocate a public display of levity, rather a quiet and private moment of appropriate humor to break the tension. It has to be done in the right frame and moment and it must not be demeaning or harm someone who is involved or present.

b. Supervisor/Organization

- Supervisors have a dual role. One is to establish that humor at the expense of others is not acceptable. The other is to find humor in appropriate places to illustrate camaraderie and fond concern for one of their subordinates or themselves. A supervisor who can find humor reflecting some action or behavior that is germane to them and funny can be endearing and demonstrate the level of humanness they possess.

- We note that humor must be tastefully done, appropriate to the moment, and not to harm others. If this is accomplished correctly it has a positive outcome on others.

14. Take care of self.

a. Individual

- While assistance is important and often times necessary, each person who experiences the effects of stress, adversity and trauma must self-engage in overcoming the negative impact on their emotions and physical health. Without self-engagement, any process is more difficult to assimilate into the healing process.

- With the right attitude, and an optimistic outlook, it is easier to recover. This is not easy, at times, and grit to tough it out requires a personal commitment to oneself.

b. Supervisor/Organization

- Supervisors also carry the responsibility to assist an employee under their charge. While this may be in conflict to other related duty requirements, balancing the two can be accomplished. One need not compromise duty and responsibility with compassion. Understanding the dividing line and being totally open and honest are good tools to use when facing this dilemma.

- The organization, too, has the responsibility to help an employee who is experiencing issues and problems. The time for this to happen is as a preventive model heading off a problem before it occurs or worsens. We do not invest enough time, effort and resources to prevent employees from being overwhelmed with stress and adversity. The traditional model of "suck it up and move on" has no place in today's world, where the level of trauma is often over the top for people working in emergency services.

15. Take care of others.

a. Individual

- One of the great services you can provide to peers and other agency employees is to help when problems arise. Assistance must be with sincerity, honesty and without any self-aggrandizement.

- Comfort is given simply by making a call to determine how someone is, if there is anything you can do to assist, run errands, and look after needs of other family members. We often assume that when an incident is over that healing is instantaneous. It is not! Depending on the depth of trauma a familiar and friendly face is a huge dimension of comfort that can lead to reduction of stress and gradual return to health.

- There have been many instances where more than one fellow employee joined together to do such chores as cut grass, go grocery shopping, help with other physical tasks that cannot be done by the injured party. A few hours of regular help reduces cost, increases feelings of well-being and removes additional worry. What a great gift!

b. Supervisor/Organization

- The first duty of a supervisor is to care for those under his or her leadership. This means holding people to standards, to meeting the mission and goals of the agency or performing their duties in an exemplary manner. It also means that when problems arise to step up and take the lead in insuring conditions do not get worse.

- People who report to a supervisor often consider that individual the closest person in the organization to whom they relate. Given that, who better to step up to the plate and make sure all bases are covered with the level and type of assistance needed (and that includes health, domestic, property, and other influences on the life of a person who is unable to step up and care for them him or herself), than the supervisor!

We often gloss over the impact of the work we encounter and wonder why so many issues arise and different behaviors come into question. What is more serious is that this knowledge is generally received with disdain, for everyone knows officers must be tough, shake off the negative, and all will be well. I differ with that philosophy, as exposure, over time, leads to negative outcomes.

Stories abound in the human services field. Every officer with any time on the job knows of friends and others in police and public safety services that have self-destructed. The incident is then handled as a disciplinary issue and the curtain is drawn on past occurrences that were ignored by supervisors and peers, signs and issues that were observed but not addressed. An unwillingness to address small issues may lead to larger problems down the road.

Supervisors are obligated to take care of their subordinates and to address issues that detract from performance. It does not have to become a major concern if the incident is minor, but acknowledging that the supervisor is aware and offers some conversation is appropriate. Few instances of officer misconduct suddenly appear, as most incidents have a history and were known by peers, supervisors or others (Lumb & Breazeale, 2003[63]). Officers do not work in a void, they are part of an organization, they have responsibilities to peers and certainly there are many others outside the job to whom the individual has ties (Lumb, Breazeale and Colaprete (2009:18), stated: "*Ignoring personnel issues until they reach a critical stage will result in embarrassment to the individual, the organization, and the police and first responders themselves. The realization that most personnel problems were observed, but left to manifest, suggests a new approach is needed.*"

Interventions are important. People who apply them must be skilled, trained and have relevant knowledge in appropriate measures and not fall on a supervisor/subordinate role where power or intimidation is the approach. It generally forces the aberrant behavior underground and does not resolve the issue. Interventions include employee assistance programs, peer counseling, and discipline, most of them not achieving the desired changes. When professional services are needed, officers fearful of stigma or lack of confidentiality attached to that method generally will not go. Consideration of the type or seriousness of misconduct may trigger policy guidance as to what can and will be done. Most of the minor infractions are overlooked and yet, reflection of past events points to the need that some action should have been taken earlier. Yet, it is well known that when an officer is accused of some infraction or more serious issue, he or she immediately erects a barrier against further attack, consults with the Union representative and begins to construct

---

[63] Lumb, R., & Breazeale, R. (2011). Addressing Correctional Employee Behavior: The Importance of Attitude and Personality and the Role of Coaching in Facilitating Change. *The Correctional Trainer*, IACTP, Spring, *5-15*.

defenses. This impacts on performance and relationships until the problem is resolved and in many instances lingers on into the foreseeable future.

Applying Resilience Factors.

<u>Accumulating Negative Residue</u>

Public safety practitioners are not immune. They experience burnout, fatigue, depression and posttraumatic stress disorder. Prominent signals will be apparent with employees suffering these maladies. With increasing stress and accumulating negativity there is a breakdown in the human immune system that affects physical and mental health. This leads to behavior problems, ineffectiveness, decreased job satisfaction and feeling that equate to a loss of social support. This growing and lingering weariness destroys motivation, feelings of well-being, and leads to dysfunction. We all have worked with colleagues who display symptoms that are recognizable. If left unattended, they often result in tragedy.

<u>Functioning Amidst Chaos</u>

During times of high stress, usually accompanying intense and non-routine encounters with severe weather, high risk situations, danger that is over the top such as encountering someone with a weapon, a fire burning out of control, sustaining injury, a disaster scene that is overwhelming and other examples, leave residue with the individual. The need for a resilient response demands the depth of those skills to be adequate, a personal fortitude to bring them forth, and sustaining a level of courage to work alone or with others to bring the situation under control. An example is:

The original call from the State Police Dispatcher reported a traffic crash with one vehicle. Almost immediately dispatch reported there were injuries involved. Arrival at the scene of the crash revealed three dead and one alive, the driver, who was seriously injured. Two of the dead were brother and sister, visiting Maine with their family and out with friends. All were young,

One of the deceased was sitting in the back seat of the convertible, holding a can of beer in his right hand. His sister, lying on the ground, appeared to be asleep, but on examination, she had expired. The third deceased person was in the front passenger seat and he appeared to be sleeping also. Beer cans, both empty and some opened were in front and back seats. The visible images of injury that one would expect were not present.

The Trooper attending this vehicle crash had encountered many fatalities in his career, but this one was different. In reflection as to why it was different, it seemed that finding three deceased at the scene of a traffic crash, none with any visible signs of injury, was most unusual. Their almost peaceful repose was observed and mingled with sadness of the deaths, along with the realization of how even a minor crash can be fatal. These many years later, the faces and body positions, by-standers and other police officers are as clear to this former Trooper as if it happened yesterday.

That Trooper was this author. To this day I can see the bodies, the peacefulness of death, yet its tragedy as two families would return home from vacation minus two members. Needless, yes, but with commonality to the way youth live and behave. The excitement of freedom, of doing something forbidden and, in this case with terrible outcomes. The image stops motion: the bodies, the gathering crowd, the slow motion response by myself, EMTs, other police and fire fighters, all of whom were caught in that moment of time, so clear in my mind. I wonder how many others that were present that day feel the same?

Applied Resilience

You previously have and will encounter events that are so challenging they evoke fear and confusion. When all those about you are in panic or afraid to the point of inertia, you must perform and perform well. Chaos breeds more chaos and in that confusion each of us responds in our unique way. For some it is sitting down and being incapable of functioning. Others seek a path out of the maelstrom, while First Responders automatically drop into a zone to choose and activate a response compatible with their training and experience. How is this done? What allows this group to overcome the danger and threat and to perform their duties? Is there something special about them with regards to courage, or commitment, or duty?

Training and experience merge and combine with skills and knowledge, bringing to the forefront a response built on practice and experience from other situations. The grit required to persist is brought to the forefront and it strengthens positive change. It is during this period of first awareness and resulting reaction, personal resilience and finally completion of the engagement before them, that is harmful in the long-term (if not injured physically) and managed if the appropriate knowledge and skills are within.

Fortifying Personal Resilience

Researchers Maddi & Kobasa (1984)[64] proposed the concept of personal "hardiness" to manage stressful circumstances. They argue that a person should acquire a self-perception of: (a) commitment (to family, friends, work, colleagues and other engagements), b) control of (emotions, activities, behavior) and in (c) find renewed interest in what is important to them, and to (d) get involved and (e) avoid feelings of alienation. In this manner they influence the course of events they engage in and are not self-viewed as victims of circumstance.

Hardiness training engages cognition (thinking), emotion (feelings), and action (response) in coping with stressful and traumatic circumstances and events. We must be able to self-assess what is taking place within ourselves and to strengthen personal

---

[64] Maddi, S., et al. (2009). Hardiness training facilitates performance in college. The Journal of Positive Psychology, 4(6). 566-577. Routledge Publishing

endurance and resilience when danger, threat, and engagements in chaos challenge us.   To take control of your life and manage it well is a positive philosophy.

Chapter 8
Helping Others
Weighing in – Before the Fuse is Lit

Introduction.

The role of traditional police and first responders is on providing a wide variety of services that are specific to the agency's role, that one call will bring the employee face-to-face with enforcement of the law, responding to calls for service, dealing with crime, violence, accidents, medical issues, and all manner of complications where disorder, chaos and stress are often present. Their focus is outward beginning with that first call for help to the agency.

We know that stress accumulates and over time, acquiring symptoms and then transforming itself, in some cases, to the often overlooked status of Post-Traumatic Stress Disorder (PTSD). This knowledge must lead to a parallel concern for officer/responder well-being, not from those calls normally considered dangerous, but rather from what takes place over time in the thinking and behavior of the officer/responder. This falls squarely on administration as they have overall responsibility for the employees of the agency. While it is often uncomfortable for police or first responders to speak openly of their emotions, their overall mental health or to admit to serious changes in their thoughts, including self-harm or suicidal thoughts, is not only dangerous, but is poor management care of ones' employees.

Programs that help with prevention, educate employees of the outcomes of excessive stress accumulation such as increased sick leave, citizen complaint, a change in behavior and attitude and other variables that are often addressed, are an important step in prevention and intervention. Such programs are not optional, as the loss of an employee due to stress related issues is costly, as is replacement either of the person or to provide additional overtime costs. Not to mention the costs related to therapy, medication, hospitalization, etc., to those whose symptoms occasionally lead to suicidal gestures or death.

Leadership is all about employee well-being, as is the delivery of services. This takes a different focus, one that says, "*Your health is important to us and we have implemented the following programs and policies to insure we are providing the right amount of care and support.*" When in place choose to make it important and enforce compliance.

It all comes down to the value and worth of our employees. When we care about them, it includes not only visible harm indicators, but the more subtle and obscured aspects of human beings as well.

Cost of officer and first responder illness, injury from accident or encounter, and from delayed response to stress, adversity and trauma is no less harmful, and requires having programs in place to address the issues. We are in a situation where the culture may consider mental health not applicable, but research supports the opposite.

1. <u>Waiting for change to occur is foolhardy.</u>

The following question was posed to a room of police executives: *"How many of you know of an officer that self-destructed in his or her role while on duty?"* Literally all hands were raised. A second question asked: *"Of those officers, how many fall into the category this was the first time of any indicator of a problem?"* Only a few hands were raised. Seldom is a police officer, who engages in an incident where they behave outside of policy and end up in difficulty by stepping off the narrow path for the first time, directed toward the appropriate support or training in order to avoid future problems. What typically happens is that there is a gradual escalation toward personal issues. A citizen files a complaint for behavior unbecoming a police officer: an assault and battery complaint is answered with the officer using excessive force, or some other improper legal procedure that should not have occurred. But, the officer's zeal to take action was not proper procedure. There are other examples that we read about or see on television, such as stealing or lying.

Peers, supervisors and administrative personnel may be aware of an officer's misconduct, but choose to say nothing, under the premise that it will soon clear itself and that 'Tom' will be back to normal. However, Tom does not return to normal and in most cases the behavior continues or worsens. The outcome that brings it to the attention of the organization, the media and public is generally serious enough to warrant suspension, discipline or in some cases arrest. Careers are damaged or ruined, the department suffers from the stigma and questions are asked of administration about how such an incident could ever happen.

<u>EXAMPLE</u>

Warren, a police officer for the city of Charlotte, N.C., told officers that he worked with that he suspected his wife was cheating on him. He would ask them to cover while he drove out of his patrol area-- and out of the city-- to check on his wife and his residence. His peers complied and covered for him, while complaining amongst themselves of his paranoid behavior and demands on them for extra coverage while he obsessively dealt with his marital issue. Soon enough a confrontation with his wife led to a call to the County Sheriff for a domestic violence dispute, with two Deputies responding. Seeing that it was a city police officer, the Deputies told him to tone it down. No report was generated as he agreed that he would. While off duty in his personal vehicle, traveling on the Interstate with another police officer from a different community, Warren refused to pull out of the passing lane and was flipping the bird at a vehicle behind him who was trying to pass. The driver of the rear vehicle was an off-duty North Carolina Highway Patrol Officer. The Trooper recorded the tag information and looked into it further. Once he determined who was driving the other vehicle that "flipped him off," he made an informal complaint to the Charlotte P.D. The offending officer's Sergeant gave Warren a verbal "ass chewing" and told him to straighten up. Again, no formal record was made and no further review conducted to see if change occurred.

This same officer, again when off duty, was involved in a property damage vehicle crash with an elderly woman in another vehicle. The driver of the other vehicle called her husband, who worked a short distance from the accident, and he came to the scene. Before on-duty officers arrived to take the report, an argument broke out between the off-duty officer and the woman's 65 year old husband, resulting in a fist fight. The officer's punch broke the other man's jaw. At that point, Warren loaded the injured party in his damaged pick-up truck and drove to the local hospital. Arriving at the Emergency Room entrance, he directed the injured person to *"Go in there and have his jaw fixed"* and drove off.

However bizarre this story seems, it is true. Investigation led to the officer being suspended, charged with assault and battery, and he was eventually fired. The same investigation disclosed other issues that had not properly been resolved and that reveals that no supervisor intervention ever took place. It was a fiasco of the largest proportion and the ensuing law suit and associated costs were very expensive.

2. Warning signs to employee issues.

To the trained observer, there are often signals that something is wrong with a fellow employee. As a first line of defense, supervisors should be trained in the art of observing and providing correct intervention, prevention and support to their supervisees. Supervisors must undertake a caring and interested approach to their employees. Getting the job done is important but all too often the focus is only on executing the duties expected, with no consideration for the person who is carrying them out. We expect each day will mirror the last and that our employees will move forward without hiccup or roadblock. We learn not to see that which we do not want to see, or where experience has never indicated a problem exists.

Life is filled with change; not all of it is positive. Many police officers who experience a problem, one that weighs heavily on their psyche, routinely push it aside, burying it to avoid the conflict and expecting or hoping it will pass in time. Affected by a negative or life-changing incident, work suffers, behavior changes, productivity diminishes, negative attitudes emerge and other manifestations occur, displaying themselves in subtle, or obvious, behavioral or emotional changes for the individual.

Waiting for change that will return the individual to normal often allows time for conditions to worsen. Hoping that whatever is bothering the individual will pass and ignoring closer observation, will likely cause a situation to become untenable. Not paying attention and avoiding taking appropriate steps to address issues and provide help is derelict and offers little in the way of corrective measures.

As a supervisor or a caring fellow employee, when warning signs are apparent, make note of what you are seeing. Record in a private notebook the details, for depending on memory at a later time is generally not a good approach. Seek to record reasons or account for what is happening, as it helps define and work through what may be initially unclear. Note performance behavior, a negative attitude, withdrawal, increasing anger or short temper and other manifestations that are abnormal to the individual. You need to understand with some clarity before making decisions on what to do. Approaching the employee without sufficient information often serves as a prewarning to the employee that trouble may be approaching and he or she seeks a less visible role to avoid further issues.

The goal is not to accumulate evidence to attack and crush the individual's behavior, it is to help move in a direction that will bring about positive change. This requires patience, preparation, understanding and planning.

3. Approaching the employee.

Often negative employee behavior is met with a gruff, "*Straighten up Max, I don't want any more problems from you!*" That statement, given in a variety of word combinations, generally does not help much. The goal is to include the employee in problem solving, in seeking positive change, creating a collaboration to bring about positive outcomes.

If a discussion or counseling is needed, the supervisor should select a time and place to approach the employee, creating a space where uninterrupted conversation can take place. It should also be set up in a non-threatening environment. Roll call is not the time or place, for example. Privacy and confidentiality are primary keys to earning trust, along with sincerity and honesty.

Key Features of a Collaborative – <u>Leader</u>

A strong collaborative leader is often identified by the following seven characteristics. Note: These are not in order of importance or priority.

1.

Less focus on role & more on function.

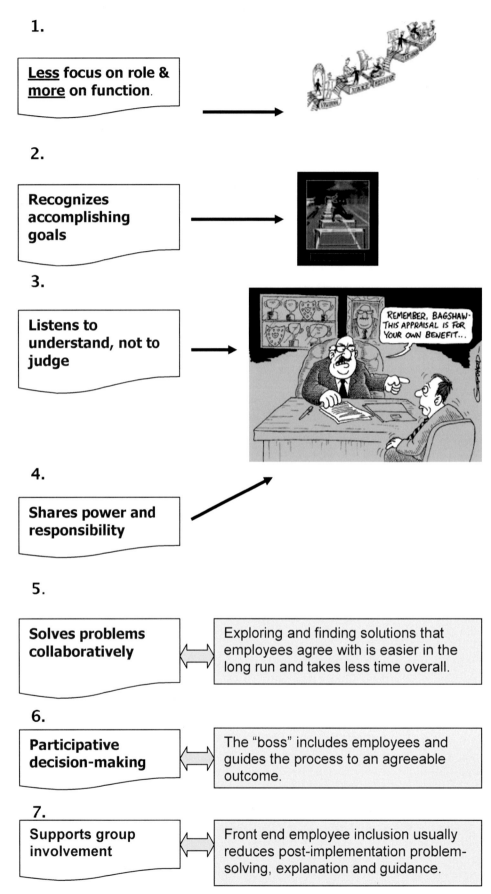

2.

Recognizes accomplishing goals

3.

Listens to understand, not to judge

REMEMBER, BAGSHAW- THIS APPRAISAL IS FOR YOUR OWN BENEFIT...

4.

Shares power and responsibility

5.

Solves problems collaboratively

Exploring and finding solutions that employees agree with is easier in the long run and takes less time overall.

6.

Participative decision-making

The "boss" includes employees and guides the process to an agreeable outcome.

7.

Supports group involvement

Front end employee inclusion usually reduces post-implementation problem-solving, explanation and guidance.

Situations Where Collaboration is Used

1. Situations where collaboration is used.

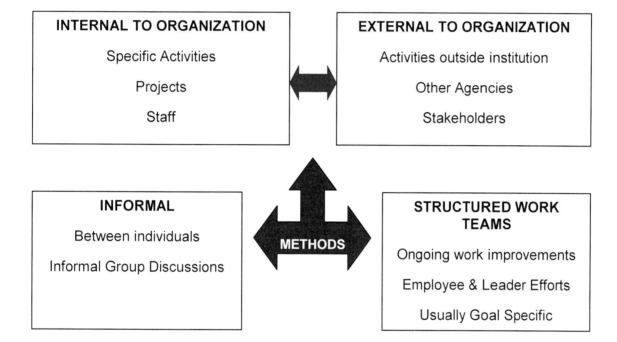

EXERCISE

Identify a collaborative situation you participated in and identify it as follows:

Question	Response Focus
1. What was the collaboration about?	1. internal 2. external
2. Was the focus internal or external?	1. internal 2. external
3. Formal or informal activity?	1. internal

	2. external
4. Who was at the table and why?	1. internal
	2. external
5. What was the outcome?	1. internal
	2. external
6. Has the decision remained successful? If yes, why? If no, why?	1. internal 2. external

Strategies for Successful Collaboration

1. <u>Involving Employees in Decision-Making Requires</u>:

   A. Sharing of power and authority

   Question: What are examples of "sharing power"?

   _____

   _____

   B. Open exchange of information

   Question: What does this mean to you – give an example?

   _____

   _____

   C. Dispersed responsibility and not central to one person

   Question: What is the strength of this?

   _____

   _____

   D. Accountability for actions and work produced

Question: Is accountability evenly distributed in your unit?

_____

_____

2. <u>Administrative concerns may include</u>:

A. Fear the loss of control. The need to know, control and be involved in decisions and to direct employees is a strong force.

B. Confrontation and justification with employees. A challenge to one's authority or position, not able to accept criticism or dispute,

C. Address other challenges to authority. Once the door is open it is difficult to shut. Empowered employees accept a greater role and insist on it. Once this occurs, employee empowerment is perceived as diminishing supervisory rule and authority.

D. A need to personally engage. If you allow employee empowerment and sharing in decision-making, it should be tempered to prevent trivial issues from being introduced.

3. <u>Key to Successful Employee Involvement</u>.

A. Remain goal focused. Do not allow distractions or lapses.

B. Define the decision/s to be made in clear and concise language.

C. Determine what skills, knowledge, and expertise are needed?

d. Determine who should be involved. Selection of people by their skills that match the task or duties to be fulfilled.

E. Determine a realistic schedule to complete the tasks?

4. Continuum of Employee Involvement in the Decision-Making Process,

Note: This is a process and is situational. Not all decisions can or should be a group exercise. The situation is a strong determining factor of the extent to which a leader can include others and to what extent inclusions might take.

Continuum

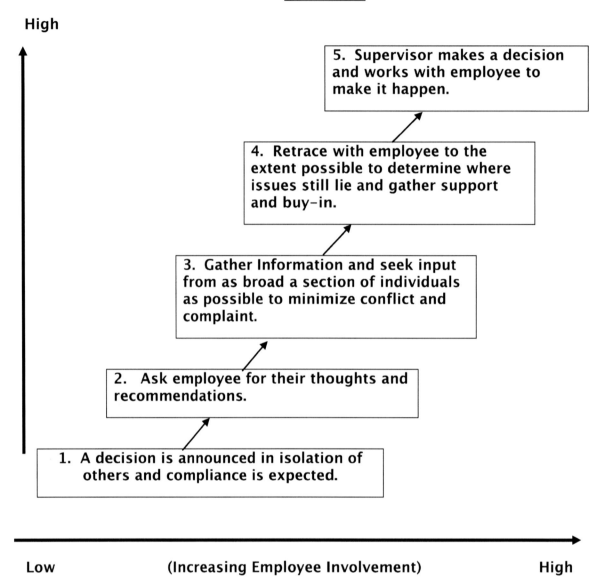

High

5. Supervisor makes a decision and works with employee to make it happen.

4. Retrace with employee to the extent possible to determine where issues still lie and gather support and buy-in.

3. Gather Information and seek input from as broad a section of individuals as possible to minimize conflict and complaint.

2. Ask employee for their thoughts and recommendations.

1. A decision is announced in isolation of others and compliance is expected.

Low   (Increasing Employee Involvement)   High

Definitions of continuum:

Discussion of each typical behavior one would observe, the rationale behind such behavior, and how it might be changed.

1. **A decision is announced in isolation of others and compliance is expected.** A decision is made by someone in authority and employee is expected to comply, to make the decision happen, and to do so without complaint.

2. **Ask employee for their thoughts and recommendations.** That input is gathered and used in making the decisions that are forthcoming.

120

3. **Gather Information and seek input from as broad a section of individuals as possible to minimize conflict and complaint.** This personalizes it more and generally, with people used to working together, creates a less contentious atmosphere. The information is considered as part of the final decision-making process.

4. **Retrace with employee to the extent possible to determine where issues still lie and gather support and buy-in.** Going back to those who will be impacted by a decision of some consequence, allows time to gather information in response, to gather support and acceptance and to insure that all members of the group are well informed and understand.

5. **Supervisor makes a decision and works with employee to make it happen.** At this level the supervisor makes some decisions based on his or her knowledge and experience and establishes timelines, conditions, reporting, evaluation and other checks to insure that the goals are being met.

5. Engaging employees in work related decisions:

Qualities of Effective / Ineffective Decisions.

Qualities of Effective Decisions	Qualities of Ineffective Decisions
• Are goal focused • Build trust and relationships • Consider everyone's interests • Separate personal ego from issues • Enable participants to learn something along the way • Provide back and forth communication among all involved • Provide positive outcomes: outcomes surpass expectations • Give people on all sides of the issue some satisfaction • Result in positive feedback from colleagues and/or superiors • Provide an acceptable level of comfort for most people	• Action based on anger or fear • The erosion of trust and deteriorating relationships • Consequences that are difficult to undo • A focus on symptoms with ignored underlying issues • Preconceived notions that dictate the decisions

6. Collaboration is key. Obtaining employee thoughts and allowing them to ask questions, reduces defensiveness, push back and complaint. Employees often have valuable thoughts that enhance a decision and reduce tension among them.

II. What is Collaborative Decision-Making?[65]

1. Definitions:

Collaboration simply means "to work together." Collaboration allows as few as two individuals to work together toward shared goals with shared responsibility, authority, and accountability. Collaboration is not about power and is not tied to hierarchical positions (rank and authority). Rather, power is linked to knowledge and expertise.

Decision-making is a process of reaching a conclusion based on one or more activities such as: thinking, discussion, exploration, fact gathering, analysis, reflection on experience and others.

Public Policy Decisions refer to actions taken within governmental settings to formulate, adopt, implement, evaluate, or change policies. These decisions may occur at any level of government.

Ask yourself the following questions as a way to judge effectiveness of a former group action.

Provide an _example_ of a collaborative group effort you were involved in:

   a. What was the _purpose_ of the group's meeting?

   b. What were you charged to accomplish?

   c. Who was selected to participate and why?

   d. What issues were encountered that had to be overcome?

   e. What was the intended outcome?

   f. Was the outcome expectation met?

---

2. Why Leaders & Supervisors Need Collaborative Decision Making Competencies.

A. The need for an interconnected organization.

While there are many component parts to the organization (facilities, roles, hierarchy, responsibilities, etc.), it is _one system_ and one organization with a common mission.

---

[65] . Reference. Campbell, N. (2005). _"Correctional Leadership Competencies for the 21st Century: Executive and Senior-Level Leaders."_ NIC.

Therefore, it is critical that the component parts reflect the composite whole. In accepting this, it is equally important that all factions see the parts as a whole. Through collaborative decision-making the organization is made stronger, more cohesive, and more effective. It is not an easy accomplishment, at times, but effort should be made to make it so.

Summary.

Employees experience a lot of stress and trauma in their daily work. The issues are many, their repetitiveness is tiresome, and over time one wonders if there ever will be a lessening of deviated human behavior. With so much focus on others, it is easy to lose sight of oneself. This same aberration applies to supervisors also, whose outward focus may diminish the needed observation of their subordinates, noticing when help might be needed and making the inquiry.

While the military has been proactive to address Post-Traumatic Stress Disorder (PTSD), the civilian side is less progressive, actually experiencing a substantial amount of denial. The preference for civilian first responders from this author's perspective is we are working with Accumulated Stress, Adversity and Trauma (ASAT). We have passed the time when administrative focus is needed to address their employees' needs within the framework of psychological, physiological and emotional needs. The constant focus to events and people, who are not members of the organization, often diminishes the need to look internally as well.

Programs that address employee education, prevention and available services are important. They give choice, support and make the statement that we care about our employees. These programs must not be optional, if we value our employees. Leadership is all important, for it manages the provision of services, provides support and seeks to keep the employees both physically and mentally healthy. Is there anything more important?

PART III: Pathways to Sustainable Change

Chapter 9
First to Last Day on the Job

Introduction:

Acceptance of a public safety career is filled with possibilities and excitement. All the images that led you to the job are within reach. The mixture of joy and intense desire to 'get going' dances about in your mind. A lengthy process has ended and now a new beginning awaits you. It is freeing, exhilarating and no thoughts of negative outcomes fit within that moment.

I. Starting the Career.

Decision to do this work.

People come to the decision to do this work from many points of view and with a wide range of expectations. Becoming a first responder may be a lifetime goal or it may emerge from a conversation with a friend, past military experience, a family member who works in the field already, or any number of influencing factors; including a strong desire to serve the public. The important point to consider is whether or not you possess a clear willingness to enter into the profession by taking the necessary steps to apply and jump through the many hoops required to complete the final goal, which is never far from your mind. Of all the reasons a person chooses this path, few ever consider the danger inherent in the job. Danger from exposure to the limitless behaviors you will encounter, the deviance, the hostility, the anger and accompanying aggressive actions. The devastation of arriving at a fatal accident; the deep sorrow or despair that comes with working with humanity across the lifespan, from birth to death. All of these are guaranteed to take a small piece of your overall sense of well-being. But, that is what awaits you in the future. Nonetheless, the joy of beginning your new career, your new life as a first responder, is not lost on what "may be" at some later time.

Determining what the job is all about.

Television is not the best source of what policing, fire, correction's, EMT and other important first responder jobs do. Highlights of exciting and quick solutions are great in 30 minutes, but the reality of every job varies for numerous reasons. With each passing day we learn new aspects and fit them into our thinking, feelings and responses. The newness of the job brings repetition and routine, along with flashes of the unexpected. A long road lies ahead and one's path and longevity are dependent on variables not considered early in the career. As experience and exposure to events multiply, we soon have an understanding of what is expected and what we generally will be doing in our new roles.

Are you Compatible with the Role and Responsibilities?

The initial roles of (excitement is not a role) helping people, catching bad guys, addressing structure fires, responding to medical emergencies, checking for law violation and dozens of other duties, help you begin to identify some of the negative aspects of your new job. There are things that make one uncomfortable, angry, frustrated, and curious. You may find that you get bored with the same old behaviors, only the faces changing. You may find that no matter how hard you try, some people and situations never change. On average, five years or more into the job people find it is difficult to imagine leaving, even though during the tough times there is a strong pull to do just that. The negative aspects of the job seem to outnumber the positive. You feel both trapped and thankful to be doing something that is unlike most other occupations. Negative life experiences deeply affect us. When they are apparent, as they quickly become so in the first responder world, you need to give serious consideration to how you can, and will, survive the stress associated with your new role and responsibilities. You need to be prepared to ask yourself this question: are you ready, able and willing to work your way through the hard and often dark times? Do you have what it takes? Can you hold on to the good things that happen in your new role, and let them be enough to get you through the bad?

II. Influence of other Internal and External Sub-Cultures.

What to Expect.

The world of public safety and first responder services separate us from other occupations. We have the power over mobility, freedom of discretion, and the ability to make decisions that literally can make the difference between life and death. We realize that as first responders, not everyone may like us and that we will be held apart from many aspects of society that others enjoy or take for granted. The public can be judgmental, critical, and have unrealistic expectations of us. When voiced publically, such criticism can weigh heavily on us--for a moment or more, becoming selectively compartmentalized. Internally, issues of role, rank, structure, duty, friendship and trust also end up holding much space within your psyche. Finding a way to sort it out and make sense of it all, can be a challenge.

External expectations may well depend on who is involved. The community looks at general public safety and other first responder services as needed and valued until it negatively affects their life, expectations or demands. During those moments you will have to face the conflict and find ways to diminish how it sometimes negatively impacts the citizen(s) you are serving. You will learn those special skills and tactics to use in reaching a peaceful resolution with some of the negative people that you encounter, and move on. In other words, you will learn how to put such negative encounters, and there will be many, in a place that does not allow your life to be negatively impacted.

Others that you work with will tell you their stories and offer up their complaints, making you aware of actions being taken or failing to happen on the job.

All of which will direct and influence how you think, feel and act as you find your way in your new role. Some of these influences will be short term and others of longer duration, where it may become more deeply personalized and integrated.

The influence of others, whether they are in leadership positions over us, or equally our peers, can be powerful. The key is not to lose sight of ourselves, our feelings, thoughts; our values and the essence of our being. We often get caught up in the plight generated by others and "go along" because it is expected. This stems in part because we are of the same occupation and peer group, and from the simple peer pressure fact that not supporting others is considered unacceptable. Unions, peers, loyalty and other reasons all act to direct behavior. The key is to rationally weigh facts, consider how you feel, what makes sense and appears to be an appropriate action (based upon your training and experience) and have the strength and will to carry it out.

In the field of first responders, the concept of being a self-directed leader can take great courage. It does not mean that we step outside of our assigned role to "take over" and assume responsibilities that are not ours to take on. What being a self-directed leader means is standing strong within yourself by having the confidence to know who you are as a person and as a provider of human services? It means that you must not lose sight of who you are and what you value and stand for as a person In the midst of turmoil on the job, making clear decisions is not always easy. Sometimes it's important to find a place of solitude to weigh out facts and carefully reflect on the matter at hand is important, especially when facing critical decisions or in solving difficult problems. It is not foolish to depend on one's self, when appropriate, even though the outcome of the decision-making may upset others. The ancient saying, "To thine own self be true", says it all. There will be times in your career that you will need to stand strong as a self-directed leader—to stand for what is right, to have a voice, when appropriate, and to do the right thing in the moment it is called for.

Let facts guide your actions. What you do <u>not</u> know <u>is</u> harmful to your mental processing. Seeking solutions from a place of ignorance can only cause further problems. When in doubt, gather as much information as possible by drilling down to the level necessary to acquire all you need. Missing information leaves a hole in the problem you are trying to solve.

III. Self-Determination.

<u>Managing Peer Influence</u>.

When it comes to the more personal relationships that are developed with peers in the work place, your emotions are often the motivating influence that sways our actions. Emotions alone should never be the sole motivating influence, for that very reason. Issues affecting one person or a small group can morph into a major gripe or complaint. When someone is impacted negatively, it is a natural reaction to seek others to stand with us as we grouse and demean others. It is a natural reaction to push back when something is unacceptable or not within our ethical beliefs about right and wrong. The stronger the voices, the more likely overcoming the opposition becomes, at least in our mind. Too many people leap on the wagon and display support for issues that are often wrong, not correctly conceptualized or improper for the moment. If you have a message that is clear and offers an alternative path, speak up (be the self-directed leader that was previously discussed)! We do not have to challenge, just offer rational and clear discussion as a solution is sought. The quicker we resolve a problem the faster people return to work and lessen the pressure of the situation.

Determining Your Career Path.

While not cast in stone, many who make it for several years in public safety tend to remain through to retirement. There is movement within the field from organization to organization, through promotions, job changes and taking on new responsibilities that add to the normal demands of the job. And realistically, we should be more proactive rather than taking each day as it happens and hoping for the best. We can influence outcomes rather than wait to see what will happen. For example, you have aspirations to go from patrol to investigations. Rather than wait for an opening and applying with hopeful anticipation, take a bit of your off-duty time, seek permission, and spend some time with the people that serve in that division. This is not to be overbearing or a pest, but to learn, know and be known, and to demonstrate your enthusiasm and display a mature approach to displaying your future interest.

Planning your career path is an important matter to consider, even at the beginning of your career in the field. While you cannot put exact dates to milestones, you certainly can map out a path you want to follow, a tentative timeframe that will allow you to not only work, but to continually seek self-improvement. It is helpful to seek advice and guidance from others that you know and will get to know and respect. It is always helpful to one's career when you seek the input and influence of those with more knowledge and experience. It's important to keep track of your own career path by including dates and notes on important events, training and accomplishments in order to allow your perception and your career planning to remain on track.

If we commit twenty-five years to our career, we should take responsibility for the direction we set and work to meet those milestones. We are not totally dependent on others, as we have control over many aspects of our career, and we should match our motivation with the actions and steps that move us to the outcomes that we desire. . This is not done in isolation of others, but with their help and input However, you shoulder the greater burden and responsibility in working toward creating a positive journey toward your goal(s) in your chosen field.

IV. Helping Others and Resisting Influence.

Individual Roles within a Complex Organization.

Once we step into our role as a first responder, it won't be long before the job we hold soon involves others as colleagues, friends and a multitude of other working relationships. Quickly the relationships can become greater than the jobs we do. Our awareness of the larger peer group includes all manner of nuance, most of which has nothing to do with our work, yet it can quickly become difficult to balance. Those with whom we work with daily often share their issues and needs, and many of us will do the same in return. This knowledge opens the door to feelings of support, agreement or disagreement, willingness to argue and complain, with much of it being held within the group and not taken or spoken to supervisors or administrators. When we find ourselves stepping out of the job we are assigned and minding all manner of other issues and concerns, we engage in aspects of workplace drama that is not ours to participate in. This diminishes productivity, distracts us, creates conflict and dissention and disrupts us from staying on the path that should be directed by our role and responsibilities.

What to do When You See Dysfunction.

Workplace drama is not uncommon. It is a product of people, events and discrimination about what is and what should be, at least in our thinking. The natural tendency is to spend valued time bitching about the condition or situation and not taking steps to achieve positive change. When dysfunction is occurring, giving some thought on how to bring it under control is not just the purview of someone else. If you work there, you should invest some time and energy to help create the best working environment possible, regardless of limited change influence from those in leadership positions.

Without being abrasive and with a sincere interest in offering positive suggestion, consider solutions that your experience and knowledge indicate will have the potential for positive change, and share them with someone in a position of authority or who has the ability to assist with problem resolution and change. Discussion and sharing of ideas may well result in appropriate outcomes. The point is, positive attitude and constructive thoughtfulness may well culminate in desired change.

You also can work with others who may be inclined to being argumentative by using persuasion and thoughtful suggestion to build support for changes. And, when shared with the organization's administration, may result in positive outcomes. The goal is to build a positive environment without adding to the negativity. Turmoil, regardless of the degree or depth, is disruptive to performance, harmful to psychological and emotional systems and rarely achieves the outcomes desired. We have some control in managing our personal attitude and actions.

Chapter 10
Organization and Personal Safeguards

Introduction:

Safety and well-being must be a conscious effort, made by the individual and the organization, in partnership and with mutual support. For far too long, personal well-being issues, dealing with exposure to extreme stress, adversity and trauma, has taken its toll, as illustrated throughout this manual. The "*tough it out*" or "*just part of the job*" mentality should be deemed contrary to common sense and how we judge the worth of our employees. No excuses should ever be accepted In regard to the safety and well-being of employees.

While organization-wide responsibility rests with the agency head, it falls to each employee to do their part as well. One suggestion is to insure that supervisors take the lead with their group of employees. There are several aspects to the supervisor's role that should positively impact the emotional well-being of employees. They include:

- Knowledge of signs and symptoms of emerging stress and adversity.

- How to address issues and problems with the individual or group.

- Establish discussion groups with employees to review and understand problems.

- Review stressful situations and discuss outcomes with those involved.

- Promote health and well-being, including emotional issues and problems.

- Help when asked, engage when necessary and maintain trust and confidentiality as you assist an employee back to balance. This may require outside professional assistance.

The supervisor and employee discussion group will form the core of individuals interested in promoting emotional health. This group will also undertake planning to address issues, and educate themselves on the effects of stress, adversity and trauma as it affects life-style, health, work performance and relationships.

Education and knowledge can lead to the formation of a sophisticated program that is designed to help fellow officers who are experiencing stress and other debilitating pressure. It will not be easy, given the culture and the protective silence the officers wrap themselves in. However, history shows us that we have lost a lot of good men and women because the effects of accumulated stress results in dysfunction and the onset of problems; problems that could have been avoided or helped through the support and intervention provided by groups like this.

Making emotional health a priority.

Creating a peer coaching support group to examine and address issues of harm that emerge from exposure to accumulated stress, adversity and trauma (ASAT), removes some of the stigma around the topic of mental health[66]. Statistics on the harm that can be and is done, clearly points to the need for elevated organizational concern with this aspect of the job. The peer group can do the following:

1. Schedule a "building resilience and endurance" meeting in a place offering comfort and privacy.

2. Have refreshments available.

3. Have a designated facilitator from your group.

4. Have an agenda that lists discussion – topics.

5. Engage in general discussion of stress and encountering adversity.

6. List steps to reduce and lessen the effects of A.S.A.T. and ask if anyone will discuss if they have used any of them.

7. Identify needs the organization can address and plan to bring them to administration.

8. Schedule a second meeting and select one of the 'building resilience" topics that the group will discuss and explore how it can be applied using specific examples from past encounters.

See the following book:

Breazeale, R., & Lumb, R. (2013). *Resilience Building: Peer Coaching.* ISBN-10: 1492812447 & ISBN-13: 978-1492812449. Amazon Publishing.

Note: Police and first responder organizations should host meetings that are informal and for the purpose of addressing stress, adversity and strenuous conditions and calls. In most normal situations this is not the case. Debriefing of critical incidents is generally done post-incident. This is helpful for a number of reasons and serves to support on-going programs. Employees can also conduct more informal meetings and develop a program that is focused on the needs of those who are experiencing high levels of stress and emotional concern. Employee meetings should take place in a comfortable environment that is conducive to a discussion about emotional and

[66] Breazeale, R., & Lumb, R. (2014). Resilience Building: Peer Coaching Manual. Amazon Publishing. ISBN-10: 1492812447 & ISBN-13: 978-1492812449..

performance issues and concerns that are more often than not ignored or "hidden" from the outside perspective. During the group meetings, the emotional and psychological health of employees is being discussed in a non-threatening and supportive session.

As part of the discussion it is a good idea to remember that the impact of A.S.A.T. is not only on the individual employee (first responder), but also lays heavily on family members, friends, colleagues, peers and other social groups, with relationships in all areas often becoming strained. Solutions will emerge to existing problems if the group provides regular meetings, consistent support, creates at atmosphere of confidentiality, caring and genuine interest in each individual's well-being. The peer coaching program educates employees about the effects of stress and adversity and presents techniques and strategies to help overcome personal trauma.

Reducing the effects of stress and adversity

A. Organization. The organization cannot and must not abdicate responsibility for its employees believing that because they hired someone who was deemed psychologically stable and therefore acceptable for police and first responders' duty at the onset of their employment, that this same employee's psychological (mental) health will continue to remain stable after 3, 5 or more years of service.

The question is: Is it realistic to assume that all staff will be at the same level of emotional and psychological stability after being on the job for a number of years, as they were when they first entered their position? The type of life a civilian experiences, in comparison to police and first responders, is vastly different. The general public does not have to encounter danger, threatening situations, motor vehicle and other type of accidents, domestic violence, threat of personal injury and the potential for death, all on a daily basis.

The individual, prior to employment, was probably not subjected to the deviance that people act out when they harm, murder, attack and do unmentionable things to others that are deemed illegal. As previously mentioned, while physical and protective equipment is of the highest quality, the reality is that there is no other "armor" to protect the first responder from emotional injury than that provided by the aforementioned support groups and opportunities. Psychological well-being becomes a concern when the employee does something in violation of policy or displays behavior that comes to the attention of the larger organization or even becomes a public issue. Performance is the common element and that emerges from one's thinking. This concern includes safety to the individual's body and emotions, psychological well-being, and concern for the amount of stress and adversity that is encountered. It is often couched in concerns for liability and negative publicity, prompting official statements directed to the problem and a guarantee that the situation is being handled.

This is not sufficient! We cannot assume that an employee exposed to the level of negativity encountered over many years will not be adversely affected. Screening and a data recording system should be maintained to identify an employee at risk and then offer appropriate help to overcome the issues and realign the individual in a new wellness model. Prevention programs that strengthen an employee's durability and ability to confront and work through situations that are stressful, adversarial and threatening are critically important. The tools needed to help the individual are necessary for supervisory officers to properly assist employees under their direction.

B. Supervisors. Supervisors are critical in the matrix of employee wellness. As a first measure they must be well themselves. Caught up with self-related issues is distracting and prohibits expending sufficient time with their subordinates. Commitment by each supervisor is critical to the success of the program.

C. Partnership with external services. Awareness of programs that work well in other organizations will help to develop your agency's program. People in public and private organizations that have similar programs are generally willing to share information and to engage with public safety and other first responder organizations to help them develop and emerge successful in reducing the effects of S.A.T.

D. General Attitude. Fostering an attitude that recognizes vs. turning a blind eye to the inevitability of first responders experiencing negative effects of S.A.T., over time, is in itself healthy. Doing something about it is even healthier. One must foster the philosophy in the organization that says, "We are concerned and want to do something about it!" is by far better than opening an Internal Affairs complaint.

Reference Information.

An Employer's Guide to Workplace Emotional Wellness
June 2011

National Business Group on Health
20 F Street, NW, Suite 200
Washington, D.C. 20001
202.558.3000 • Fax 202.628.9244
www.businessgrouphealth.org

The purpose of this guide is to educate employers about the business association between organizational practices, personal resilience and the emotional health of its employees and dependent.

Of importance from the "An Employer's Guide to Workplace Emotional Wellness" are five recommendations for workplace emotional wellness programs, services and culture support. They list the following in the above cited report. They would be a strong inculcation into any organizations' planning and practices.

Recommendation #1: Help employees build and use personal skills to take responsibility for their emotional wellness.

Public Safety Application.

- This must be an organizational wide project. The agency has a responsibility to create programs that every employee can benefit from them.

Recommendation #2: Integrate emotional wellness with general medical and wellness programs.

Public Safety Application.

The initial hiring conducts wellness, physical health and psychological testing. Wellness, physical health and psychological testing should be conducted at mandatory time frames for all first responders, with results being reviewed by supervisory staff, ongoing. Referrals for individual and/or group support for psychological test results that reveals deficits or areas of weakness/concern should occur and also is monitored.

Recommendation #3: Align the corporate culture to incorporate workplace emotional wellness.

Public Safety Application.

- Emotional wellness is absent from discussion, policy, training and focus of attention. This drift often includes a distant consideration, but generally never enters the minds of most.
- A change in culture will take time, but is it any less important that all other considerations?

Recommendation #4: Facilitate transparency, communication and support for a corporate culture of emotional wellness from executives and managers.

Public Safety Application.

- The concept of emotional wellness must reach from the newest to the oldest employee. Unless we have "total" belief in emotional wellness, we are creating an illusion.
- No employee must be exempt. The goal of wellness is laudable.

Recommendation #5: Remove actual and perceived barriers to emotional wellness programs and service.

Public Safety Application.

- Myth, tradition, culture, belief, and other influences create a situation where we ignore signs and symptoms. When someone self-destructs we wring our hands and wail about the sad state of affairs. We contribute to it if we fail to remove the barriers and provide the additional level of support needed.

Summary.

The safety of organization personnel must be paramount and strictly enforced. This is an internal act that says to each employee, we value you and want you to be safe and secure in your work. Left to the individual, we know that lack of response is all too common and people wait until it is too late...and they self-destruct. When it is too late to help someone, we must assume that supervisors and organization failed in their duty.

The last behavior needed is one that reflects on employees. The average new first responder is going to be feeling the pressure of the job from day one. Peers and other messages often result in their feeling the need to suck it up and move on. Simply moving on from stress, adversity and trauma is, as the United States military discovered after years of denial, that simply moving on also bring all the baggage with you. That very thinking has contributed to many negative personal and professional issues and accomplished little in helping the individual return to a healthy balance in work, life and attitude.

Safety and well-being must be a conscious effort by the individual and the organization, in partnership and through mutual support. While this is a clear mandate, it is nonetheless not common. We provide all manner of safety equipment to keep the person safe, but ignore his psychological, emotional, physiological and social side. Getting out of sorts with self is difficult enough. Add to that a loss of support by supervisors and administration and we have a serious situation bordering on melt down, or worse.

Establishing a peer coaching health program to inform employees about the effects of stress and adversity and present techniques and strategies to help overcome personal trauma, is unquestionably needed. Like bullet resistant vests, reinforced cruisers, and equipment for safety of personnel, an emotional wellness program and mentality all points to the "We care about our employees"!

Chapter 11
The Value of Understanding Emotional Intelligence

Introduction:

We are concerned with the plight of police and public safety officers and first responders in general. Why? Because the very nature of their work has a high potential to diminish their emotional well-being, resulting in a life style riddled with numerous encounters with stress and adversity[67]. Traveling this career path, as mentioned in previous chapters, also involves family issues, financial struggles, etc., where personal disarray often emerges from years of experiencing on the job, unavoidable, stress related events.

Within this occupational group the potential of acquiring a deviant societal outlook, that considers people as corrupt and views the world as being filled with criminals, where no one is to be trusted other than those who have traveled the same path exists. A career spent immersed in society's problems, investigating violence, providing care and custody to people who victimize other humans, responding to dangerous and intense situations and being an observer of the worst in society, corrodes the officer's sense of right from wrong, and dulls their ability to focus on personal safety and well-being. The journey takes its toll, one day at a time. As the years pass the once robust and healthy officer is burdened with numerous physical and emotional issues that erode his or her life and those of family, friends, and peers far quicker than other careers.

When we examine an officer's psychological health, the expectation is to be tough, show no emotion through the toughest of circumstances, buck up and move forward without complaint. Decades of evidence suggest this attitude or approach to policing in general is simply wrong, and most often results in ill health, emotional trauma, marriage and family destruction and other negative outcomes that debilitate and create lasting damage. Post-traumatic stress is typically associated with military confrontation in battle. However, it is a disorder that is often found in the field of police and first responders, as well.

Understanding and utilizing emotional intelligence.

To overcome the effects of stress and adversity in the field of public safety and first responders one must acquire new and improved skills in both recognizing and understanding the effects of emotion on the individual and how, when knowledgeably and effectively managed, such skills can be useful in positive ways. Herein lays the

---

[67] . Lumb, R., Breazeale, R., Lumb, P., & Metz, G. (2009). Public Safety Officer Emotional Health: Addressing the Silent Killer. (Reprinted) American Jail Association, March/April 2010, XXIV (1), 8-20.

importance of understanding the meaning, role and connection between emotional intelligence and stress, adversity and trauma.

Emotional intelligence, simply stated, allows a person to recognize his or her own feelings and those of others. Learning about emotional intelligence, and understanding how to apply it in our daily lives and work, allows us to not only motivate others but also how to effectively manage both the emotions in ourselves and with other people that we engage with.

The very use of the word "*emotion*" triggers a negative reaction in the strongest of men. Yet, our emotions are one of the most primitive and baseline operating systems that humans possess. In dangerous situations for example, the primitive emotion of fear will provide the adrenalin to react appropriately, and save a/our life. The more common term for this is **"fight or flight"**

We know that emotions are a routine part of our daily lives. The question is: what do we allow others to see and what do we keep below the surface, and why? Emotions are many and varied in intensity or frequency. Emotions are subject to change given a situation, past experience, or other variables.

Table 10.1
Emotions People Display

Happiness	Stressed	Hate Hesitant
Sadness	Perturbed	Confused
Anger	Panic	Desperate
Fear	Pity	Indifference
Annoyed	Horror	Exhaustion
Complacent	Bemused	Anxious
Frustrated	Love	

Different types of emotions represent "*potential*" responses that arise during a particular situation or circumstance. We seldom consider how we get through the day managing ourselves and knowing that some of what we are feeling cannot be displayed or allowed out of the privacy of our mind. For the most part, we do not like to display our emotions (or do we?) when others are around. This is especially true for people who work in and with the public.

Our emotional control center, and home to our personality, is located in the brains frontal lobes. This area of our brain is involved in the following activities:

Table 10.2
Brain Activities

1. Motor function	Raising arms, walking, bending, etc.
2. Problem-solving	Reasoning and considering what we know
3. Spontaneity	Those unanticipated actions – laughter
4. Memory	Recall and associations
5. Language	Speak one or more languages

6. Initiation	"Hey john, want to go for lunch?"
7.Judgment	Right from wrong, take action or not
8. Impulse Control	Refrain from angry outburst
9. Social	Interactions with people
10. Sexual Behavior	Flirting; dating; intercourse: verbal talk; rape

Understanding Emotional Intelligence:

Research and application of emotional intelligence (EI) to decision-making, behavior and performance has shown to be extremely positive to the individual and those they associate with. When we understand other people's motivation and performance, we are able to work with them in finding common approaches to needs.

Emotional intelligence is defined as the capacity for recognizing our own feelings and those of others, motivating and managing emotions to guide thought and action. It helps to understand the difference between one's mind (reasoning, cognitive processes) and heart (emotions). When in dangerous situations, for example, we need to be calm and to consider alternatives, safety procedures and other cognitive processes.

Emotional intelligence is a learned capability and helps guide performance. It is also a critical component central to leadership and helping others to do their job more effectively. A good leader is able to tune into how others are feeling and thinking, to read the impact of a decision or action required of others and to respond accordingly.

The U.S. Navy utilizes emotional intelligence training to improve leadership and personal command style. Some of the outcomes of that research found that superior leaders do/have the following qualities:

 ➤ Balanced a people oriented personal style with a decisive command role,
 ➤ Did not hesitate to take charge, be purposeful, assertive, and businesslike,
 ➤ Were more positive and outgoing,
 ➤ Were more emotionally expressive and dramatic,
 ➤ Were warmer and more sociable (smile, friendlier, democratic, cooperative, fun to be with), appreciative and trustful,
 ➤ Task oriented and firm in expectations.

Mediocre Leaders displayed the following traits:

 ➤ Taskmaster
 ➤ Legalistic
 ➤ Negative
 ➤ Harsh
 ➤ Disapproving
 ➤ Egocentric
 ➤ More authoritarian and controlling
 ➤ More domineering
 ➤ Tough-minded
 ➤ Aloof and self-centered

> ➤ Led by the book
> ➤ Legalistic and inflexible standard (e.g., Movie "Mr. Roberts").

According to the Emotional Intelligence model, there are five components[68]. They are:

Competencies	Application
1. Knowing one's emotions 2. Managing emotions 3. Motivating oneself	How we manage ourselves.
4. Recognizing emotions in others 5. Handling relationships.	How we handle relationships.

The first three are categorized as competencies which determine how we manage ourselves, while the last two are those which determine how we handle relationships. Under the first component of EI (Emotional Intelligence), – knowing one's emotions – we are focusing on a true self-awareness, or recognizing a feeling as it happens. A greater sense of self-awareness provides the ability to make more realistic assessments or our own capabilities and self-confidence, which channels us to better decision making.

Jack Welch, Former Chairman of General Electric said,

> *"A leader's intelligence has to have a strong emotional component.*
> *H/she has to have high levels of self-awareness, maturity and self-*
> *control. H/she must be able to withstand the heat, handle setbacks and*
> *when those lucky moments arise, enjoy success with equal parts of joy*
> *and humility."*

Working with others in community safety and preparedness is not about oneself, it is about blending the many philosophies, scope of knowledge, ideas, feelings and emotions into a cohesive and forward focused planning and goal achievement effort.

2. Major Researchers' views on Emotional Intelligence (EI):

A. **Reuven Bar-On**[69] stated that EI is an array of non-cognitive capabilities, competencies and skills that influence one's ability to succeed in coping with environmental demands and pressures.

B. **Salovey and Mayer**[70] (creators of the EI term) said the ability to perceive emotions, to access and generate emotions so as to assist thought, to understand emotions and emotional meanings, and to reflectively regulate emotions in ways that promote emotional and intellectual growth.

---

[68]. Rosene, R. (2005:14). Naval Leadership Assessment & Development. U.S. Army War College.
[69] Bar-On, R., Oarker, J., & Goleman, D. (2000). The Handbook of Emotional Intelligence. Amazon.com books.

[70] In Stein, S., & Book, H. (2000: 14). EQ Edge. Stoddart Pub.

C. **Stein and Book**[71] provide the following indicators of EI.

- A set of skills that enables us to make our way in a complex world.

- The personal, social and survival aspects of overall intelligence, the elusive common sense and sensitivity that are essential to effective daily functioning.

- Street smarts and common sense.

- The ability to read the political and social environment, and landscape them; to intuitively grasp what others want and need, what their strengths and weaknesses are; to remain unruffled by stress; and to be engaging, the kind of person that others want to be around.

- The capacity for recognizing our own feelings and those of others, for motivating ourselves, and for managing emotions in ourselves and in our relationships. It describes abilities distinct from but complimentary to, academic intelligence, the cognitive capacities measured by IQ.

D. One View: Five personal competence components & accompanying sub-components:[72]

Table 10.3
Personal Competence Components

Self-Awareness	
Knowing one's internal states, preferences, resources, and intuitions	
1. Emotional awareness.	Recognizing one's emotions and their effects.
2. Accurate self-assessment	Knowing one's strengths and limitations.
3. Self-confidence	A strong sense of one's self-worth and capabilities

❖

Self-Regulation	
Managing one's internal states, impulses, and resources	
1. Self-Control	Keeping disruptive emotions and impulses in check
2. Trustworthiness	Maintaining standards of honesty and integrity
3. Conscientiousness	Taking responsibility for personal performance
4. Adaptability	Flexibility in handling change
5. Innovation	Being comfortable with novel ideas, approaches, and new information

❖

---

[71]. Stein, S. & Book, H. (2000). The EQ Edge. Toronto, Canada. Stoddart Pub.

[72]. Five. New York, NY. Bantam Books.

Motivation	
Emotional tendencies that guide or facilitate reaching goals	
1. Achievement Drive	Striving to improve or meet a standard of excellence
2. Commitment	Aligning with the goals of the group or organization
3. Initiative	Readiness to act on opportunities
4. Optimism	Persistence in pursuing goals despite obstacles and setbacks

❖

Empathy	
Awareness of others' feelings, needs, and concerns	

1. Understanding Others	Sensing others' feelings and perspectives, and taking an active interest in their concerns
2. Developing Others	Sensing others' development needs and bolstering their abilities
3. Service Orientation	Anticipating, recognizing, and meeting customers' needs
4. Leveraging Diversity	Cultivating opportunities through different kinds of people.
5. Political Awareness	Reading a group's emotional currents and power Relationships

Social Skills	
Adeptness at inducing desirable responses in others	
Influence	Wielding effective tactics for persuasion
Communication	Listening openly and sending convincing messages
Conflict Management	Negotiating and resolving disagreements
Leadership	Inspiring and guiding individuals and groups
Change Catalyst	Initiating or managing change
Building Bonds	Nurturing instrumental relationships
Collaboration and Cooperation	Working with others toward shared goals
Team Capabilities	Creating group synergy in pursuing collective goals

E. Emotional intelligence has been described as "an array of non-cognitive capabilities, competencies and skills that influence one's ability to succeed in coping with environmental demands and pressures" (**Reuven Bar-On**). It can be illustrated by the following descriptors:

- Set of skills that allows you to make your way in a complex world
- Personal, social and survival aspects of overall intelligence
- Common sense
- Sensitivity essential to effective daily functioning (street smarts)

- Ability to read the political and social environment
- Intuitively grasp what others want and need
- Other peoples strengths and weaknesses
- Remain unruffled by stress
- To be engaging (the kind of person others want to be around)

Applying emotional intelligence.

The following is helpful to apply to similar situations in your experience. They offer a view of what can be helpful to our personal health and well-being, and *that* responsibility begins with the individual.

1. Know and understand yourself first. What makes you do what you do and what is the rationale behind these motivations? You can be clear on helping others when you are able to articulate clearly the values and goals you have set and when asking others to help.

2. When you reach out to a community, you are asking people to buy-in and to believe in your vision and reasons for the request. This requires your being able to appeal to their needs, to see ahead into a future that is not present and where some of the ideas being presented might not be within their grasp. You become a salesman.

3. Respect for other opinions and ideas. When we engage people we must be willing and able to understand their thoughts, blend them with ours and seek a common and workable forward motion. With agreement come increased motivation and commitment. Building community capacity to prepare for natural and man-made disasters or other emergency situations is partially on faith and partially on solid planning. Working with others requires engagement in both.

4. Social skills, talking, listening, resolving issues, identifying and solving problems as well as other mutual understanding is not always easy. We must be willing to engage from an honest position and work with others, accommodating their needs and ideas as well. This will, in time, result in achievement of the established goals.

5. Collaborate with others. Who else needs to be present to offer expertise, ideas, resources and willing participation? We recommend starting with existing services, those individuals in the community with expertise, training and established roles. This includes Fire, Police, EMS, Emergency Management and others at local, county, state and federal agencies. It is also important to identify people with expertise in the community who will offer this knowledge to the working group. This includes all manner of people including medical, energy, construction, and others who will be identified.

The short of it is, our vision is to recruit and train members of a community who collaborate as a representative cohort group to work with others who are living, working, visiting and who have other roles in their city or town, to bring them emergency preparedness and resiliency training. The goal is to plan ahead, to foresee when an emergency might arise, and when it does, for affected citizens to be able to respond appropriately, sustaining life and safety to the extent possible.

Sub-cultural influences within the work organization are created by the internal ecological environment that develops over time and represents many levels or layers of the organization[73] (Allen, 1985). Danger encountered in the job is a factor in police officer attitude as is his or her acceptance or rejection by the police subculture, an important marker to the officers job related health and well-being[74] (Stratton, 1981). While common mission, values and vision statements exist and are the guiding organizational principles, we find a variety of sub-systems at work that identify specific groups or functions, each with their own cultural norms. Culture and sub-culture is influenced by many variables, some of which inhibit change while others are motivators of transformation. Programs that promote positive change and address needs and issues within an organization are important to the mental and emotional health of the organization.

Behavior indicators, both conscious and sub-conscious processes, usually emerge as actions, statements, and other visible manifestations of stress that are often observed by others. For some individuals, healthy activities are sought while others turn to alcohol, drugs or other sources of relief that are harmful. Tossing back a few beers after work, if habitual, may diminish perspective and attention to other matters, leading to dysfunction. It is easy to turn to engagement in activities that lead to other, bigger personal problems. Peers, supervisors and organizations have a duty and obligation to intercept and help, when able.

This must be the case if the officers' physical and psychological well-being is of primary concern to the employing organization. Programs are available to substantially reduce the effects of dealing with society's negativity, brutality and violence and its cumulative effect on the human condition (often resulting in some level of PTSD: Post-Traumatic Stress Disorder).

Assisting public safety personnel in acquiring special skills and knowledge that are useful in addressing personal needs and establishing a foundation for acquiring skills as a peer coach is a primary goal of resiliency training. Public safety is a unique occupation that provides critical services to communities. Employees are subjected to unusual and stressful situations that, over time, accumulate and result in behaviors and performance problems that cannot be left unaddressed. Addressing and reducing the effects of exposure to danger and traumatic events is a common goal of the individual employee and the organization, and demands that steps are taken to strengthen resilience and sharpen methods and skills used to help employees who may become derailed by the challenges they confront.

We should not expect that simply by telling an employee to "straighten out" that he or she will automatically do so, or possess the skills or resiliency to do so. Success for change is highly dependent on the individual and his or her supervisor, along with substantial levels of sincerity, trust and confidence. Helping employees maintain a

---

[73] . Allen, J., & Allen, R. (1985). Short term compliance to long term freedom: cultural based health promotion by health promotional. American Journal of Health Promotion. 1:39-47.

[74] . Stratton, J. G. (1981). Police stress: An overview. In L. Territo & H. Vetter (Eds.), Stress and police personnel. Boston: Allyn and Bacon.

healthy lifestyle benefits family, peers, work, and the health and welfare of the individual.

Summary.

A deeper understanding of emotional intelligence goes directly to many aspects of our life, our work, family functions and association with others in a variety of venues.

The five personal competencies are utilized in all that we do in the world we live in. When we are able to manage ourselves, we are just as capable of managing others, for in understanding comes awareness and selection of good choices. To recap and reinforce meaning, the five competencies are:

1. Self-awareness.
2. Self-regulation
3. Motivation
4. Empathy
5. Social skills

Consider them in relationship to your life to determine how they are used. It is equally important to assist our employees reduce the effects of continuous exposure to all manner of danger and traumatic event. Strengthening personal resilience is very helpful and so is a clear understanding of emotional intelligence, those five competencies in our lives that help us manage ourselves and others. We also must provide leadership to others in assisting them maintain balance in their life and work.

Emotional intelligence allows us to recognize our and others feelings and can assist us to motivate, manage emotions and find appropriate outcomes to situations and performance issues that arise from time to time. We know that emotions are a routine part of our daily lives. The key is, what do we allow others to see and what do we keep below the surface, and why. Emotions are many and varied and are subject to change given a situation, experience, or other encounter.

Chapter 12
Planning for Retirement

Introduction.

One Author's Look Back from Today

While I am not an advocate of the "looking back" concept, except as it pertains to "lessons learned", I never-the-less could not help but consider the past as I examined several timeline pictures sent via Facebook by the Maine State Police headquarters site. It brought me back to days and events that occurred well before my ten years with them, It struck me that one's "place" in life, being part of something important, is critical to who we are and how we define ourselves and the meaning of our lives.

That gives us a place to immerse both head and heart, where importance is contributing to a group that is bigger and perhaps better than who we are individually, than if we stand alone. Use of the word "group" is not random for it serves many utilities that help define structure. Group is synonymous with a depth of solidarity, a collective understanding of purpose, and it means being known to all who belong to it for its broad and unconditional acceptance of who you are as an individual, as well as who you are as a critical member of the larger whole.

An agency like the Maine State Police held great purpose for me, not rigid or unyielding, but something that each individual shared with others who wore the uniform. The MSP provided a powerful force to bond with, provide solidarity, and a fierce depth of pride that was projected by one and all. When seeing others in the field or at the barracks, there was always an awareness that we walked in the same footsteps of those who walked before us. Each step represented a long line of shared history and a way of life that dispelled chaos and brought comfort in knowing what was expected. While we were individuals, we were also part of the collective whole. Men stood side by side and faced danger. Some were injured, some were killed and many were left grieving. But seldom, if ever, did the Teflon shell that protected us, crack.

At the end of the day, when the darkness fell and others were sleeping, our heads and hearts were ever present, waiting for the call that brought us together once again to address yet another situation deferred by others. As time passes and the day comes when it is time to retire, life as we know it stops. We are propelled from the place that held us so tightly giving us definition, identify and purpose, and thrust out into a world that represents chaos and often lacks clarity. We cannot help but think of those days and times and recall the stories we each have and sometimes share. That link to the past, to the memories of those now gone and whose time and career was held dear to them and others who knew and worked with them, side by side. We still seek that group bond and camaraderie. It is more elusive now, distanced by time and other conditions, never as strong or meaningful, yet continuing to frame the story that we call life.

The police of today live in the moment. It is not always possible to see where others, serving in the same position, were at a former time. Yet, as surely as the next call comes in and response is initiated, the shadows and examples from former events are passed through, not seen, not heard, but part of the "being present" as fortified by moments of long ago. It is difficult to see back, and certainly not forward, with clear certainty. Knowing you travel, not alone but with the ghosts of the past, can be comforting. Memories of the past remain a force in life, sustaining us with links to the present and the past. A brotherhood bonded for time immemorial. Do you doubt it? Ask a former Trooper or police officer while closely looking at his or her eyes, as the past is recalled and applied to the present moment. There is a straightening of the body, a smile, a feeling of comfort, knowledge of having belonged, and continued purpose – all there for the discerning eye. It is what it is, and we are thankful.

Convergence of Time & Place.

If you live long enough, years of service and time to retire converge and suddenly you are faced with decisions that are not as comfortable as once thought. When young, the future goal of retirement is seldom thought about, it is a form to sign and a brief glance of what will be contributed to a fund that will comprise your income in twenty-five or more years. It is not given sufficient thought or planning until much later.

The twenty-five years pass quickly enough and when thoughts of leaving take hold, you then begin the financial assessment that should have been done many years before. Many are finding that they have insufficient resources in savings and retirement to live the life style anticipated. Government pension plans were hardly lucrative to begin with and with the economic downturn and legislative bodies further reducing cost of living increases, the difficultly becomes much more demanding.

US World News posted "*The ten retirement issues that are here to stay*" (April, 2011), a list reflecting current and future conditions facing the retired. In retirement, the options diminish and those that present themselves are limited. Add to that the rising costs, lowered return on investment, and unknowns such as the cost of fuel, food, insurance and other goods and services, and reasons to worry are real for sure. The financial issue is exacerbated by the emotional and mental health impact of stress accompanying a realization that usefulness, engagement, belonging and other issues not previously encountered in employment are front and center in retirement. The ten issues are:

1. Boomers turn 65 unprepared for retire. They have not saved enough money, did not invest well and are not able to plan for future costs.

2. Americans don't understand finances and investments. Thus, the efforts at saving and building capacity have suffered.

3. Huge federal deficits threaten our way of life. The plummeting value of the dollar, falling international confidence, rising deficits, job loss, companies moving overseas, and other related are beyond our control.

4. Social Security is broke and broken. Social Security Administration calculates that the program can pay all promised benefits until the year 2037. Then, its reserves will be exhausted and ongoing Social Security payroll taxes will cover only 78 percent of benefits.

5. When should I begin taking Social Security? Taking benefits as soon as possible at age 62 locks in payments that are only 75 percent of what they would be at age 66, which is defined as the full retirement age for the current wave of retirees. Delaying benefits at age 66 will raise them by 8 percent a year until age 70, after which benefits do not increase with age.

6. Get ready for inflation. Retirees must plan for inflation. This means that the buying power of fixed incomes will erode over time. It means the real return of investments, after inflationary factors are considered, may decline.

7. Look carefully at retirement fund fees. It can be very hard to determine how much you actually pay the firms that manage your retirement accounts and mutual funds.

8. Medicare cuts would ruin seniors' futures. Seniors will face healthcare challenges for the rest of their lives. Access to care will become harder to find as the nation's growing physician shortage runs smack into rising numbers of aging baby boomers looking for more care as they get older.

9. Retirees are worried about outliving their money. Just when we should be happy about regular gains in longevity, we're instead bummed out by fears that we won't have enough money if we survive to old age.

10. Low interest rates hurt retiree incomes. The Federal Reserve's free-money policy has destroyed meaningful returns in bonds, CDs, and other holdings with returns tied to interest rates.

Fantasy, absolutely not! America as we knew it has changed and will not return to its former values. We are faced with new challenges that did not exist, we encounter a level of greed that eclipses any previous stages, perhaps the former Roman Empire was worse, and the off-shoot is massive suffering and few who are listening.

Employers Must Step to the Plate and Educate Employees.

Retirement planning for our police officers, especially those who are near completion of their 25 or 30 years of service, is an important service for employees. Receiving financial, career and retirement planning is a worthwhile program for all employees as all relate to an honorable career that leads to productive engagement follows a 25 to 30 year career in public service. We cannot depend on words or agreements from earlier years as change is inevitable and often directs future outcomes. It is time for every employee to have the skills and a comfort level with financial issues of current and future living needs, to plan for that future date and to be assured that what is in place is the best possible advice that can be obtained.

There are several variables at work that lead to the above conclusion. One is the willingness for someone to engage in public service for a long period of time, a calling that truly benefits citizens. We also know that many public service roles (Police, Fire, EMS, Forest/Game, Sheriffs, Sea & Shore and many other occupational specialties, due to the very nature of the jobs they do, exposes the individual to stressful and traumatic events and situations, that overtime take their toll. A physically and mentally healthy employee is critical and career long efforts to maintain the individual in these areas too, is equally important.

Thus, hiring a person initiates a process in which the individual carries out the duties of their job, but also someone who deserves and, from my perspective, is entitled to a combination of services that not only grow them in the job they do, but prepares them to continue to offer their skills and knowledge post-retirement. They have much to offer and generally we do not tap into those skills, knowledge, abilities and experience, all of which are enhanced as they progress through their first career, in preparation of the next contribution.

Each employing agency can determine what this model might look like, conduct a trial program and consider implementation to their agency. Society will benefit with culture and social gains evident as carefully selected individuals are provided with options to personal growth and development.

Summary.

Retirement is an abrupt change of life, mentally, physically and emotionally. The very things that identified us both within our heads and hearts and from others who know us, change and it is not with the smoothness of many life transitions. Our very identity is different the day after retirement for we have divested the authority, responsibility and accountability that held us so tightly all these past years. Even those with whom we worked see us differently, not from disrespect, but that we have moved on the burden remains with them, separating and dividing what was so familiar just a few hours ago. Our thinking is clearer that we still belong, and so we do in our heads, but the remaining force sees it a bit differently. Distanced by time and other life engagements, we sleep in the reality of it all, and seek to find a new pathway, where fulfilment and purpose fill the new void.

Chapter 13
What to do When Reality Strikes

Stepping from work to retirement often raises may unexpected challenges. You no longer have to get out of bed and be some place at a specific time or expected to put in eight hours of work. You no longer have to be present and responsible to address social issues created by others. Former responsibility is replaced with a "no action required" and it leaves you feeling uncomfortable, like something is missing. Your social circle diminishes substantially and interaction with the "guys at work" instantly becomes a smaller group of family and friends. As the distance from reporting to work lengthens, the contact with former colleagues diminishes as they move forward in their work and you seek new ways to engage yourself and to feel of value.

No longer having to report for duty, individuals of make lists of things to do and over time they may not get done, even with the greatly expanded time available. There is a period of despondence or lethargy as the once high value, high excitement, and strong purpose role you had is suddenly missing. Unless you have replaced the former job with one that continues to require your interest, time and engagement, the quiet of the day becomes troubling.

Officers retire for many reasons; principle among them is the completion of required years of service. For a variety of reasons new employment is sought to replace the police job or perhaps to pursue new opportunities of greater interests. If a choice is available, remaining in the job may not be for the right reasons either, with many staying to reach retirement, having too many years invested to leave, possessing a healthy fear of starting something new, an unwillingness to lose a sense of comfort and security, or they do not have other marketable skills. There is a song that has relevance from a very unlikely source, the MOFFATTS, and it rings true, "*Reality-- if you are what you do, and you don't, you ain't!*[75] [See: Appendix B]

REALITY

If you are what you do, and you don't, you AIN'T!

If you experienced a feeling (or reality) of isolation as a police officer, it only becomes greater after retirement. If you have not developed a large number of non-police friends or have avoided participation in social groups because the label you carried was sometimes an inhibitor to building relationships. Isolation becomes loneliness if care is not taken to avoid this dark place. Your past "identity" is somehow changed. You still feel like a police officer, you still look at people with a discerning

---

[75] THE MOFFATTS lyrics are property and copyright of their owners. "You Are What You Do" lyrics provided for educational purposes and personal use only. **Copyright © 2000-2015 AZLyrics.com** http://www.azlyrics.com/lyrics/moffatts/youarewhatyoudo.html

eye, and you feel the same emotions that coursed through your veins when working the job. But there is a difference; it is no longer you they call on to respond to social issues, crime and disorder.

We define ourselves by our work. One of the most common questions asked of strangers is, "what do you do for work?" The use of "I was..." seems disingenuous because you do not feel different, but, *you are.* Your need to be recognized for your years in policing, fire, corrections, EMT, game warden and other important services is challenged. The values and goals that your former job provided need to be reevaluated. There are things that can be done toward a very achievable goal of helping oneself to return life to a healthy balance, once again. The key is to know what those values or goals are (or should be—for you, specifically), and then to seek them out.

Pre-Planning is Important

Hooker and Ventis[76] (1984, 478) note that "*Retirement, as any major event in the life cycle, requires adjustment*". Dobson and Morrow[77] (1984:81) stated, "*Retirement attitudes were more strongly related to work commitment and job satisfaction than age, sex, health, and income.*" Research also tells us that pre-retirement planning can have positive effects on post-retirement satisfaction (Schmitt and Pulakos[78], 1985). Thinking about and making plans to examine what in life is satisfying is helpful to future emotional and physical health. Bauer and Okun[79] (1983: 264) concluded that "... *life satisfaction is a relatively enduring cognitive assessment of attainment of one's desired goals or overall condition of life.*" One must identify that place within that leads you to satisfaction in retirement, not always easy. It might be with other people and groups, it may be more internal and private, but it has to be someplace. You must exert control of yourself, for failure to do this often leads down a dark path. Coming from a strong and all-encompassing work ethic and moving into retirement mode is negatively correlated with satisfaction. Thus, it is important to begin retirement planning in advance and to consider what changes will take place in your life when the final bell is rung and you no long put on a uniform and enter the world of policing that you have known for more than a third of your life.

---

[76] Karen Hooker and Deborah G. Ventis. Work Ethic, Daily Activities, and Retirement Satisfaction. Journal of Gerontology, 1984, Vol39, 4, 478-484.

[77] Cynthia Dobson and Paula C. Morrow. Effects of career Orientation on Retirement Attitudes and Retirement Planning. Journal of Vocational Behavior 24, 73-83 (1984).

[78] Neal Schmitt and Elaine D. Pulakos. Predicting Job satisfaction from life satisfaction: Is there a general satisfaction factor? International Journal of Psychology 20 (1985) 155-167.

[79] Patricia A. Bauer and Morris A. Okun. Stability of Life Satisfaction in Late Life. The Gerontologist, Vol. 23 no. 3 pp. 261-265 June, 1983.

Goldfarb (1994)[80], states that retired police officers experience a number of psychological complaints including depression, anxiety and marital discord. Add to this physiological, emotional and social issues and a large array of harmful influences can exist. Goldfarb's observations found the <u>five</u> main issues retired police officers encounter:

1. Retirement as a loss of identity and self-esteem.
2. Marital difficulties.
3. Retiring for the wrong reasons
4. Inability to plan and organize time.
5. Boredom.

Goldfarb also provided three primary factors that shape an officer's satisfaction with retirement:

a) Psychological effects of retirement,
b) Future career challenges and
c) Finances.

Within each of these categories many sub-topics lurk. Some can be harmful to your health, others can be helpful—depending on the pre-planning you engage in, or not. When retirement arrives and the world seems bright and positive, it is a good time to take stock, identify any holes in the plan and take steps to fix them, quickly! Anticipation of pending pot holes might allow you time to make plans to take a different road, thus saving yourself for experiencing a great deal of distress and upheaval.

<u>Career and Retirement Planning</u>.

It takes upward to 80 percent of one's working income to maintain a post-retirement standard of living. What was considered adequate at the beginning of a career will not be sufficient at the end, in most cases. If a second career or alternative pursuit of income is not in the cards, planning must take place or the retiree may find him or herself without adequate financial means of support. The purpose of retirement planning is to allow the enjoyment of a less stressful lifestyle and perhaps to finally do those things on your "bucket list."

New opportunities are available to many of the newly retired. If one prepares for that day, the chances of acquiring them are much higher. The employing agency also has an obligation, as discussed previously, for it should take the necessary steps to prepare their employees for the transition from work to retirement. Other organizations, such as the American Association of Retired Persons (AARP), have programs to assist with new job preparation and placement.

---

[80] Goldfarb, D. (1994). An Instrument for predicting retirement satisfaction in Police Officers: A Pilot Study. Retrieved January 18, 2003 from the World Wide Web: http://www.heavybadge.com/retire.html

Pre-retirement services by the employee's organization could include resume preparation, interview skills, how to conduct a job search, taking inventory of one's skills and knowledge and how determine if additional training or education is warranted, along with how to obtain funding assistance. The world of employment will have changed in the twenty-five years the individual has been on the job; updating is required. The employee's organization should keep a list of potential jobs that police officers could seek, establishing a collaborative partnership between the police department and public and private organizations. One should not take for granted that a twenty-five year career in policing will open many opportunities for employment. You must have requisite skills that are applicable to the time you become available to the job market, or you will find many doors closed.

We get lost in the work of public service, the organization and the routine barely noticing that years of service have slipped by and we begin to see a logical end of the long career. Your identity for the past twenty-five years was clear, not only to those who knew you or encountered you in a professional or personal way, but it is also a self-identification that you can never forget. This is evidenced with off-duty police identification being carried at all times, concealed weapon, awareness of surroundings, and dozens of other "I am a police officer" indicators that you bring to the surface of your everyday life. Your life may be centered in the role and purpose of being a police officer and suddenly you no longer perform those duties. It can lead to despair, anxiety, and other emotions that are unhealthy—unless you are prepared for them and learn how to prevent or manage them in an effort to return to health and balance. Civilian life is a strange existence. Adaptation post transition into retirement is not easy, even under the best of conditions. But you are men and women of fortitude and persist in those life goals you establish as important. It is no different in in retirement, thankfully!

What to do? Alignment of hobbies goes only so far. Other time-filling events may quickly dwindle or grow tiresome. The anticipation of getting into uniform and doing the duties associated with being a police officer are no longer a consideration, and you can become disheartened. Police departments, either singularly or in a collective partnership, should provide retirement transition services. This program would include both the officer and his or her partner or spouse, for both are affected by the pending retirement. Discussion on what to expect, how it will/can be addressed, is a first step in a transition program. Understanding that retirement can be uncomfortable and that it can also be stressful, while intuitive, nonetheless must be discussed.

As previously noted, these symptoms are not the only discomforts experienced. Prior exposure to all manner of human chaos, engagement and experience with traumatic events, and a gradual buildup of stress over the years, alter perceptions of normalcy and distort individual outlooks. Similar to the experiences of military troop, police and other first responders also experience Post Traumatic Stress Disorder (PSTD). Performance of duties becomes difficult and erratic behavior is more difficult to control. Some compensate by increased use of alcohol and drug abuse, elevated anger, increased aggressiveness, confrontation and judgmental feelings and accusation lead to marital problems and divorce. Peers begin to notice a change but are loath to say anything, preferring to ignore and sometimes cover for the aberrant behavior.

Police Officer Suicide

Unless addressed, negative emotions may worsen and an event will occur that necessitates action, which experience shows, is not positive and rarely results in a positive outcome. When these behaviors are allowed to extend into retirement, they exacerbate and sometimes erupt, resulting in serious physical or mental illness or, even worse, death due to suicide.

Police officer suicide, according to the FBI, is six times higher than the general public *and more than triple for retired officers*. Police officers who are medically retired or disabled are more likely to commit suicide than the general public. For everyone who does take that drastic action, we must ask how many others contemplate doing the same. That consideration is frightening, and the need for increased intervention and support is even more evident.

The National P.O.L.I.C.E. Suicide Foundation[81] (1998) stated that over 300 law enforcement suicides occurred in 1998. Also, more than twice as many police officers commit suicide than are killed in the line of duty. Hill and Clawson[82] (1988) examined mortality rates for different occupations and found that peace officers had significantly higher suicide rates than other occupations that involve physical danger and/or shift work.

Base responsibility lies with those closest to the struggling officer. The job is stressful and it causes deviant behavior from exposure to years of dealing with humanities worst. We cannot simply state that officers can (or should) tough it out, for we know they do not, as evidenced by suicide, physiological, psychological, emotional, and social issues that occur. Supervisors are the first line of responsibility as they are required to attend to the physical, emotional well-being and job performance of each employee. Supervisors must be trained to identify "red-flag" symptoms and act on what they observe through intervention planning and support. We do not leave our employees to their own endeavors when problems are noticed— because of the traditional expectation of toughness or the need for privacy, despite evidence to the contrary. Even after retirement, organizations need to have in place programs for their former officers. Retirement and stepping out the door to a new life should not cut the former officer off from career planning and retirement support programs or other such options and interventions.

Provide Assistance Before retirement

---

[81] . Community Policing Dispatch. (1998). "By Their Own Hand: Suicide among Law Enforcement Personnel. COPS Office, 2(4), April.
(http://www.cops.usdoj.gov/html/dispatch/April_2009/suicide.htm

[82] Hill, K.Q. and M. Clawson, (1988:2). "The Health Hazards of Street-Level Bureaucracy: Mortality among the Police," *Journal of Police Science and Administration* 16(4), 243-248.

Acknowledging that police work is stressful, that it includes frequent encounters with adversity and trauma and that it will negatively impact health, among other things, must be discussed. Departments or even training academies must develop a program for the soon-to-retire officers; one that is specific to the needs of that group of individuals meets professional standards and that will address post-retirement considerations. I speak not about a "day before" retirement packet of information; I refer to a program led by a person well skilled in discussing mental health and emotional issues and the real difficulties and challenges of retirement, as well as its' potential rewards. This may begin a year before retirement and include sufficient meetings to allow discussion and exploration of ideas, feelings, and examples and to explore the pending new reality.

The Badge of Life (http://www.badgeoflife.com/) recommends the following steps when developing a training program for its soon-to-retire officers.

1. Create a dedicated staff committed and trained to the task of working with pre-retirement planning.
2. No cost and confidential employee counseling service.
3. A contracted confidential counseling service for employees.
4. A peer support officer program. Note: They must be thoroughly trained for this role.
5. Establish a mandatory Critical Incident Stress Debriefing Program.
6. Annual interactive training on managing stress and adversity. As a career program it would have outcome effects for the soon to retire person.

Chapter 14
Finding Purpose

A sense of purpose emerges from the daily life of a police officer and other first responders. But a first responder's position also serves as a target for complaint and as a lament to the status of humanity from time to time. It also tells a story of the love of what one does in the service of others. The path takes the officer and/or first responder through many trials both personal and professional as they interface with all sides of society. Images of death, violence and all manner of inhumanity are mixed with sadness for what people do to one another. Shouts of laughter can be followed by tears that are shed for the little girl of three whose mother's live-in boyfriend, aggravated at the child's crying, slammed her against a wall breaking her neck, only later trying to lie his way out of taking blame. Images of drunk drivers who crossed the center lane and killed others, the robber who shot and killed a store owner for no good reason but hatred, and the thousands of other traumatic events faced with courage and grit, compelling the first responder to stand firm because there is no one else coming that will help.

Going to work each day includes the anticipation of seeing colleagues, engaging in the job, and being on the front line of social order (the type that intercedes in arguments, physical fighting, and other levels of life and disruption. To the common man, all first responders may appear to be "just alike," dressed in similar uniforms, driving the same vehicles, "all the same." However, as any first responder knows, behind each uniform lies strong, talented, caring human beings who are sincere in their worry and compassion for their fellow man and the course that they see humanity taking in the 21st Century. For most workers it is being within the safety of the organization, among friends and people who understand the world within which they operate, that brings that sense of comfort, belonging, and camaraderie. There is recognition by the public; even though it often represents a fear by others, a dislike, and a desire to harm innocent beings that draws the first responder back, day after day, year after year. And while there is ample griping and complaint from many who work in the field, for those who remain and have a clear vision of service, it also represents a deep love of what one does, for those whom one serves, and for the opportunity that is not comparable to any other field of public service.

To repeat a previous reference that also applies to the concept of finding meaning, Goldfarb & Aumiller [83](2008) list five of the most common complaints of retired law enforcement clients that contribute to depression, anxiety and marital disharmony. They are:

1. Retirement as a loss of identify and self-esteem

---

[83] . Goldfarb, D., & Aumiller, G. (2008). *Heavy Badge* website.

2. Marital difficulties
3. Retiring for the wrong reasons.
4. Inability to plan and organize time
5. Boredom

The sudden change from being a member of an elite government agency, the distinction who felt wearing the uniform and performing the job duties, the felt sense of purpose and the association with like others, now suddenly absent, literally one day to the next, is disheartening, to say the least! A similar issue is that once retired, those you left behind act as if you have morphed into another being, no longer a colleague, a brother or sister in arms or duties. It happens, sometimes in small steps, sometimes rapidly, but as surely as the sun rises, you will notice the change and feel great discomfort from it, among other feelings. Suddenly life holds too much time with not enough to do to fill it up. One experiences feelings of disconnection from all things known and familiar. Unless pre-planned, the retired officer has nothing of value to occupy his or her time. This can lead to marital disharmony or significant discouragement or dysfunction – for how can it not?

In Tanguay-Masner[84] (2008), they cite how a police officer's career exposed him or her to all manner of terrible events, periods of boredom to fully engaged activity, and then dealing with the same issues and problems over and over again. It gets very tiresome and disheartening; one can wonder if, in fact, they are making a difference at all. At times it seems not. While there is less research on the civilian side of police and first responder career-long stress, there are similar parallels found to Post traumatic Stress Disorder symptoms between the military, civilian police and first responders. Although the situations, people and uniforms may be different, depending on the intensity of the situation, the frequency of the traumatic event(s), or the duration, the end results—the traumatic symptoms—are often the same, varying only based upon each individual personality and experiential history or exposure to previous traumatic events earlier in their lives, before their service career began. The National Center for PTSD[85] (2008) stated that problems associated with PTSD include:

- Drinking and/or substance abuse
- Feelings of hopelessness, shame or despair
- Relationship problems including divorce and violence
- Physical symptoms (flashbacks, crying uncontrollably, feelings of despair or doom)

These same symptoms follow a police officer (and other first responders) into retirement. The worst case outcome from untreated or unrecognized PTSD is officer suicide. The FBI statistics (2008) report that suicide is six times more likely to occur with law enforcement officers than members of the general public, and may even triple for retired officers. More disturbing is the fact that officers who are disabled and medically retired (on medical disability) are 45 times more likely to commit suicide than the average person (FBI, 2008). The California Association of Highway Patrolmen

---

[84] . Tanguay-Masner, V. (2008). Solving Ethical Dilemmas in Law Enforcement. FBI Academy Class 235
[85] . http://www.ptsd.va.gov/

(CAHP)[86] claims that for medically retired officers, the suicide rate is an appalling 2,621 per 100,000.

Violanti[87] (2007), discusses police suicide from a retirement perspective, indicating that once out of the job, the retired person is suddenly removed from a feeling of security they have enjoyed and adapted to for twenty or twenty-five years and "face a conflict of emotions" (74). Retirement is generally not planned for, skills and knowledge current with the new retirement world out of date, and the requisite attitude that should accompany seeking new engagements, not present in many. There are many demons that emerge from this environment.

Like all forms of stress, adversity and trauma, it can accumulate slowly, or quickly, over time. The cumulative affect inflicts damage based on what is observed, experienced, touched, smelled, tasted, and dealt with. Human beings can inflict some of the most horrific of damage onto others. Police and first responders must face it (eventually) and deal with the consequences. Unfortunately, responders do not necessarily "fix" themselves as they should by recognizing there is a problem, seeking help, counsel or collegial support/intervention. Even more irrational is the lack of organizational attention to the problems. We outfit our personnel with the latest of gear to protect the body from harm, while utterly ignoring the emotional, physiological and psychological damage. Organizations do have responsibility for the welfare of their employees as it relates to the direct impact of their job duties. They should accept that responsibility for their workers mental and emotional health to the same depth and well-being as with physical health.

Processing a candidate for a police or first responder position requires a battery of tests that include psychological fitness and physical health. If the candidate passes these tests with all other requirements being equal, they get hired. Once hired and working across the next 20 or 25 years, generally there are no further measures of psychological or physical readiness. As time passes, the individual is exposed to and immersed in dealing with all manner of deviance, dangerous, and discouraging aspects of disorder that humanity can shove at them. This wears on one's psyche and alters one's behavior and attitude, generally not for the best.

As stated earlier, and repeated here for grounding in understanding, requiring periodic review to determine when the pressures of stress, adversity and trauma needs some assistance to bring about balance in that person's health, is seldom, if ever, done. The purpose for standards in doing these assessments is not to shove someone from service, rather to provide the needed assistance to maintain both physical and mental health during their career and to help them move into retirement, when the time comes, in as positive a manner as possible. That is not too much to expect for the services provided to the public over the decades.

There are a number of acceptable approaches to agency provision of career long care and concern for the mental and emotional health of its employees. The most prominent are Employee Assistance Programs (EAP), Peer Coaching Support, trained in-

---

[86] Badge of Life, 2008, p.4
[87]. Violanti, J. (2007). Police Suicide. Charles C Thomas Publisher.

house staff who are available to help if called on and whose role may include referral to a professional treatment person. Training in the effects of stress, adversity and trauma and the harm they can do, if not checked, is critical. This program must begin at the Academy and be applied periodically throughout their career. Discussion of emotional and mental health mindfulness, engagement in critical incident stress debriefing, and having a number of people sufficiently trained to recognize signs and symptoms of problems, is the right thing to do.

We have danced around this issue for as long as police and first responders have existed. The belief that PTSD stigmatizes or indicates a weakness and should be ignored borders on liability and disservice to the organization's employees. Like the weapon, vest, cruiser cages, and other protective gear, the individual's mental, emotional, psychological, social and physiological well-being should be of prime concern. It would be cost effective, when we add up the ancillary costs of performance discrepancies, injury, disability, social and personal costs, etc. A healthy and productive employee, who serves their community for two or more decades and then enters retirement still productive and contributing to their community, is truly a valuable asset.

Is It Time to Mourn? Recollections of a Trooper[88]

Stop the denial and implement appropriate assistance

Looking back, I am responding to a "*10-55 PI*," a coded dispatch, an impartial statement of a reported serious traffic accident with injuries. I hear the wail of the siren, the reflection of the blue lights off buildings and motor vehicles, and of other traffic pulling to the side of the road to allow my passage at a fast rate of speed.

I leave the City of Biddeford, having passed through its crowded inner city of streets and buildings and head toward Sanford on Route 111 where the "10-55" awaits my arrival. Traffic is light, night has fallen and inside the comfort and security of the cruiser, I am isolated from others whose curiosity allows them the question, "*Where is he going is such a hurry?*" I am alone with my thoughts, hearing subconsciously the police radio but I am not connected as it does not relate to me or where I am going. Traffic blurs by, the accelerating sound of the cruiser's engine, clear at this moment, as I pass others and head to a destination similar to many of the past.

Time and distance in a police cruiser, rushing to the scene of some incident, seems not separate or connected. It is the mental picture of what lies at the destination that is dominant in my mind. As I approach the accident scene, I see stationary vehicles pulled to the side of the road, a few people milling about, all uncertain of what they should do, can do, but unable to comprehend what they are experiencing as they seek to process the carnage in the street before them. One man is standing in the road with a flashlight, hastily waves me by, doing his part because not doing something-- to be immobile -- would be too difficult. In the road are two vehicles, smashed. Automobile parts, oil and debris lie all about them, steam rising from one,

---

[88] 2011 files/publishing/Is it time to mourn Recollections of a trooper

one lone headlight still blazing, the others broken and still.

Grinding to a halt and grabbing my metal case with first aid supplies of dressings, bandages, and other related material of that time, I step toward the vehicles looking for people who were involved. One vehicle is empty; the other has five unconscious people within. The doors are wedged tight because of the collision, windows broken, and a deathly silence with the exception of one child moaning. I sense someone close to me and see a man pacing back and forth, hands raking the air, muttering to himself, looking at the wrecked vehicles, then away, a side step away, but turning and coming back, only to pass by grasping his head, muttering and moving. Who is he? It has to wait: the injured are more critical and other troopers are coming.

I stick my head and arms into the vehicle, speaking to the unconscious people, saying I know not what, feeling the driver's carotid artery, no pulse, not breathing. The body feels fluid and soft as I push into the side of his neck. He does not respond. The woman in the right front passenger seat is also non-responsive, not breathing, not moving, with any discernable pulse. There are three children in the back seat, quiet, unconscious, a silence that makes you want to talk to make noise to change the awful quietness and bring people to open their eyes and respond. It stays quiet, the world at the very edge of the skin covering my body all but forgotten, it remains present, but it respects what I am trying to do, but cannot fulfill, for my skills are insufficient to the situation.

Another trooper has arrived, he speaks to me. I do not turn to look at him but hear that an ambulance, firemen and other troopers are on the way. He tells me the Sergeant has also been called and is coming. I mutter something, thank him and he goes to push back the crowd--all who want to see, but not really, a scene they find of wonderment, horror, disbelief and sadness. Why are people drawn to scenes like this? Would they not want to avoid it? Don't they know that recollection of this type is not healthy, if dwelled on too often?

One of the children is still alive, she is injured, and the others are dead. Where is the ambulance? We need to get her to the hospital, now! Frustration, desperation and awareness that I am letting them down washes over me. I feel alone with them, sad their day ended like this. I wish I were someplace else, anywhere else but here.

Stepping back to look for help to remove the single occupant who is still alive and get her to the hospital, I see that the walking man is still there, muttering and with his arms moving, always moving. Who is he and what is his story? The ambulance crew and firefighters are removing the car doors, getting to the injured girl and doing what they can as she is prepared and whisked away to the former Webber Hospital in Biddeford. I see other Troopers directing traffic, telling people to return to their cars as it is all over and time to leave. Curiosity and the human tendency to gawk at things offering disbelief and the bizarre has some pull on group behavior, but to the officers, it is a hassle that must be dealt with and hinders doing what must be done. A confrontation exists, onlookers who demand the right to remain and gawk, and police who need space and quiet to carry out their duties. A distraction from the accident, the harm and the continuing unfolding chain of events, is social reality at its worst.

It is just beginning, this whole sad accident, which was later determined to be preventable. Another drunk driver who is unable to manage his consumption and believes he is capable of driving home, as he lives just down the street.

The wandering man at the scene of the accident was driving the other vehicle. He was drunk. He crossed the center of the road at high speed and struck the oncoming car with a family of five head-on, taking lives but living himself. He was now swearing, "*Look at my fucking car! Who is going to pay for that?*" A dichotomy occurs that is the reality of the situation and the ridiculousness of that statement. Disbelief that leads to initial anger and then incredible sadness, for it cannot be reconciled. The officer, me, must move forward. To not do so would be defeat, and it is unbearable to consider.

Contrary to how one might normally react, I am not angry at him at that moment. Instead I feel disgust, revulsion and disbelief. Walking to him, my shoes seems to weigh ten pounds each, I feel tired, dirty and disconnected. Determining he was the driver, he was placed under arrest and another trooper would take him to the same Webber Hospital where the young girl lay unconscious amid a flurry of doctors and nurses. He demanded his rights, refused to cooperate, and called us vile names. His alcohol smelling breath and disheveled body enveloping us as we handcuffed him, listening but not hearing, and resisting focusing too closely on his words and behavior for fear of a response that would be wrong.

The human body has shut out sounds, smells, visual images of people, vehicles, emergency lights flashing, a cacophony of simultaneous events muted, because to allow it all to have equal space, would lead to emotional overwhelm and eventual shutdown. They begin to reemerge into awareness; time has passed, how much is not known, a focus now on fellow troopers and other police and fire personnel becoming known, while the business of writing the report waits. I remember that I just wanted to take a shower, to have something to eat, to sit quietly for a few minutes, but not now, it will have to wait. It will come soon enough.

That incident was forty-five years ago, in a time and place as real as if I were standing there today. If I close my eyes, I see it in lucid details best forgotten, but in my heart I know I honor the dead and the young girl that lived. Whatever became of her? Is she alive today? What is she doing and how did she survive the events of that day? Unanswered questions that still remain, but perhaps a reminder she would not want to relive.

Our police, fire, and today's EMTs, paramedics, modern day equipment and communications are vastly improved for emergency response. We still have drunk drivers, vehicle crashes, death and dying. Our emergency responders still have the same thoughts and dreams as I do, for they cannot ignore them or shut them off. The truth being that we are not in full control, even though we want to be.

The drunk driver who refused having blood drawn, was forced to do so by a trooper and the doctor who drew it. He was substantially over the blood alcohol limit. His case went to the Maine Superior Court where a ruling that taking the blood (against his will) was legal for a number of reasons, contributed to his conviction. I do not remember his name, the trial, or other than that he went to prison. Perhaps he lies at the center of so many other similar incidents, imprints of those moments, the disgust and rejection I felt, and apparently still feel, with bits and pieces blocked out, to a degree.

I know it has left me insensitive, at times; impatient, at times; judgmental and with thoughts of harsh punishment for people who are too stupid to act properly or those who just do not care. I know that the men and women I worked with all those years ago may carry the same burden of events too horrific to discuss, that in the quiet of the night tend to keep us awake, or bring nightmares that are confusing and cause one to sweat and to feel unsafe.

I think of events fellow officers experienced, knowing that police and first responders eventually walked away, as continuing in that role was just too unpalatable. Others died early from the effects of stress, adversity and trauma experienced with each shift of being on duty. Other symptoms, all too numerous, take up residence in the individual. They are not healthy and potentially lead to future harm. They include difficulty sleeping, unable to relax, anxiety, decreased energy, depression, anger, aggression, detachment, risk-taking behavior, irritation over small issues, and other manifestations. Other disorders are harmful such as hyper-vigilance, being difficult to approach, having a stern attitude with family, friends or colleagues, alcohol and substance abuse, being pessimistic or constantly complaining. Divorce, physiological health issues, psychological and emotions struggles - unfortunately they are all too common. We see examples of terrible outcomes when we read that a current or former police officer does something resulted in suspension, discipline, firing or prosecution. Often they live with hidden monsters that keep clawing at them, seeking release. We all should feel their plight. To do so would help us to understand and empathize with those who suffer.

We do not honor them with helpful programs and realization that the effects of stress, adversity and trauma, walk hand in hand with other symptoms that we now label as PTSD. It is one and the same, only the civilian side has yet to take it serious and do something for these men and women. That realization takes its place in the museum of my mind, among the other unresolved issues that remain mostly locked away. I keep the key to that vault out of reach, for the reality is not where I want to be.

To all of those I served with and who continue to serve today in a society just as unforgiving, impatient, and demanding of things undeserved, I have one message: take care of yourself and each other. It is a worthy mission and goal to achieve. To the sometimes forgotten families, I wish for you greater understanding and support from the organizations, as well. We have let you down, too. I It is another sorry outcome that could be—is-- preventable.

Summary.

The loss of an employee due to personal issues or behavior, torts, legal wrangles that may extend for months, the cost of replacement employees and endlessly turmoil within and without the organization is costly in terms of money, relationships, opinion, morale and other indicators that harm is occurring and diminishing overall effectiveness. Outcomes of employee stress and adversity, left unaddressed, often spiral out of control and the end result is not what anyone prefers.

The effects of stress and adversity are well known. These effects are not represented by a neon sigh flashing "warning, warning" as it is more subtle, gradual in accumulating negative baggage and with behavior and attitude changes. Signs of employee disquiet are first observed by peers, later supervisors and after some calamitous event administration becomes aware. The early intervention opportunities have passed and the organization is now in a "reaction and preservation mode" and opportunity to fix the problem generally diminished. Waiting for the wrecking ball to strike can be offset utilizing an internal program with focus on prevention and balance. Developing a peer coaching skills program, utilizing selected employees, is a positive and early intervention model.

The level to which an organization addresses the harmful effects of stress, adversity and trauma through prevention and intervention is disproportionately low. The tendency is to rely on policy and discipline to prevent incidents from occurring. There are improved methods available.

The reality of harmful events, better known as PTSD with military personnel, is just as real in public service occupations. It just takes longer to manifest itself. Years of exposure and dealing with all manner of deviance, threat and danger, eventually takes its toll. It is real, it happens every day and we are not doing near enough to address issues in a positive and preventive manner.

To accept that our officers and personnel do not trust or want this protection should be overcome with justification of the reasons why it is important, assurances that the purpose is the health of the individual and to some clandestine method of weeding people out of service. All of that is possible if people put their mind to it. The damage continues and must we wait until the situation is so harmful that the obvious is accepted? I think not!

We often identify ourselves and others by the type of work that they do. This is common as it offers a glimpse into who we are and what we do and that may speak to skills and knowledge, interests and placement in the social strata, Work is important for other reasons as well and include colleagues, purpose, belonging, and a sense of achievement; not to mention salary, benefits and protection.

We find safety in association with others who are similar in many ways. We soon become familiar with other employees and take comfort, feel safe, and understand that others are in like conditions and it leads to solidarity. We recognize others and are recognized for who we are, also a symbol of comfort.

The sense of belonging swings toward change when the decision is made to leave and take on other life events. That may include retirement, job change, or for health reasons. It is not long in coming before feelings of disconnect take place, leaving you with a sense of disruption, of being on the outside and it all has a different feeling to it. The old saying, "Too much time on my hands" becomes all too true and for many it is disliked.

It therefore becomes important for an organization to have strong programs in place that assist the retiring person prepares for that change. Stepping out the door on retirement day literally may mean it is not accessible the next day. It is a culture shock, a sense of betrayal, a feeling of loss and with creeping realization of loss. The issues of stress and trauma emerging from the job remain in place and may even exacerbate, given the changed situation the person finds him or herself in.

Chapter 15
Helping Others Manage Stress, Adversity and Trauma

Recognizing Symptoms & Situations

It is important that we help others with whom we work to overcome the effects of stress, adversity and trauma. When we identify a problem, we should not wait to see if improvement occurs, nor tolerate behavior that is potentially inappropriate. Accumulated stress often results in heightened over-reaction to events, especially when resistance or push-back occurs. This often results in negativity and often with consequences that further exacerbates the person's negative behavior.

It is a cluster of custom, culture, loyalty based and other occupational rationale to ignore or overlook aberrant behavior by someone we work with, as it fits nicely in the "code of silence." We should support our peers-- there is no doubt that we are each other's first line of defense and support. What is troubling is the extent to which we pursue this silence when help is obviously needed. When someone we care about has reached a limit of tolerance and the expected next event could lead to suspension, firing or prosecution, we have waited too long. It is of particular importance that supervisors do not sit back and hope for the best. It is your job in the first instance and duty in the second.

It is never pleasant to confront someone, as we more than likely will get pushed back. When observations are such that a clear picture is formed and we have substantial fact to support what is being experienced; it is time to appropriately have a discussion. This conversation does not have to be accusatory or where you "take over" from the individual, relieving him or her of all responsibility for themselves. There are positive steps that can be taken. The following section reviews highlights of addressing behavior and performance problems.

Public safety agencies spend considerable resources recruiting, selecting, and training individuals to become police officers. Research on police and public safety job stress and accompanying performance[89] issues, demonstrate that many negative changes can and do occur and may include burnout, loss of enthusiasm and commitment (cynicism), increased apathy, substance abuse problems, divorce, and many other social, personal, and job-related problematic behaviors. In addition to reducing proficiency in performing duties, stress contributes to a variety of health

---

[89]. Performance, for purposes of this research, refers to the legitimacy of police activities and expenditures as they relate to community wishes and police performance. Drawing on Bayley (1994:96-101), the following information describes how we consider police performance. Bayley categorizes performance as the distinction between direct and indirect measures. Direct measures indicate what police activity has accomplished or achieved in the community. Indirect measures account for what the police have done but not whether there has been any effect on the quality of life in the community. Indirect measures are easier to collect and report than direct measures. He further distinguishes between "hard" (measure objective change) and "soft" (measure subjective change) indicators. See Appendix A.

problems such as heart attack, weight gain, insomnia and gastric conditions leading to absenteeism and early retirement. These are costly consequences to the individual officer and the department, and may create liability issues and other factors that reduce organizational effectiveness and hinder the development of new policing programs such as community policing.

We also know that excessive stress and adversity can lead to an individual experiencing the following psychological, social, physiological and emotional outcomes:

- Mistrust
- Avoid engagement in stressful events
- Retrenchment and stubborn responses
- Negative impact on family, friends, and peers
- Overreaction to events and agency mandates that are disagreed with.

Other issues of concern arise on performance and productivity. They include:

- Behavior that is disruptive, argumentative, sour and angry statements
- Actions that may be liability issues
- Required discipline to address policy violations
- Morale issues where others are negatively impacted
- Public confidence reduction toward the individual.

We have known for many years that certain characteristics of police officers (as an example) such as emotional stability and self-sufficiency are related to positive job performance (Diehl, et al, 1933[90]). We also know that other personality characteristics, such as cynicism, which Niederhoffer [91](1967) defined, as "*a loss of faith in people, of enthusiasm for the higher ideals of police work, and of pride and integrity*" is associated with negative job performance. Niederhoffer (1967) identified cynicism as a "major problem" with respect to police community relations. Although some authors may believe that the occupational choice of becoming a police officer might be dictated by certain aggressive or authoritarian needs and that they may intensify under stress, a number of studies (Fenster and Locke, 1973[92]) have demonstrated that neuroticism is not a major characteristic of police as a group. It is clear, however, that people who work as police officers undergo certain personality changes over time because of the job itself (Adlam & Villiers, 2003[93]; Beutler, et al, 1985[94]; Chandler and Jones[95], 1979;),

---

[90] Diehl, et al, 1933 Diehl, H., Paterson, D., Dvorak, B., & Longstaff, H. (1933). "A personnel study of Duluth policemen." Bulletin. Employment Stabilization Research Institute, University of Minnesota, 2(2), 24.

[91] Niederhoffer (1967) Niederhoffer, A. (1967). *Behind the shield: The police in urban society*. New York: Doubleday.

[92] Fenster, C. & Locke, B. (1973). "Neuroticism among policemen: An examination of police personality." Journal of Applied Psychology, 57(3), 358-359.

[93] Adlam, R., & Villiers, P. (Eds.). (2003). Police leadership in the twenty-first century: Philosophy, doctrine and developments. Winchester, UK: Waterside Press.

and that many officers level of cynicism increases over time (Abbot, 1986[96]; Niederhoffer, 1963).

The impact of exposure to stress and adversity has an effect on emotions, physiological, psychological and social behavior that is harmful to individual well-being. Addressing the manifestations associated with stress and adversity is part of the training program to help other community members. One of the more successful ways to improve the situation is to become a coach, a person who is willing to work with others to turn them around. Coaching is not for everyone, but in many instances it can and does work extremely well.

At the heart of coaching is the unique relationship you have with someone. You can create an environment of mutual trust and form alliances and partnerships with others that you work with. Creating confidentiality and not violating trust enables you to provide honest feedback and do so in a way that is not harsh or condemning.

Coaching Consists of:

1. Coaching helps people adapt to and consider the benefits of change. We are people who cling to habits and comfortable ways of life and when alteration is on the horizon, we often look for reasons not to change.

2. Change helps people focus on where they should be and not where they are given the change that is potentially in their future. Change often requires increased awareness and information to help bridge current knowledge with future information. The need exists to weigh out options, to consider positive and negative aspects and to reach a decision based on good information.

3. Coaching assists people to look at and self-evaluate how they can reconcile who they are as a person with skills, knowledge, abilities, attitudes and experience and what makes them happy and to see that successful transformation may be advantageous. In the workplace, where change is often occurring, coaching is used to show that people can better fit within the pending changes and to emerge successful. Coaching is best applied at the pre-contemplation stage of change (see the trans-theoretical model of change).

4. The coach's role is to provide support and help individuals develop an action plan. Pointing out ways for the individuals to help themselves, to find sustainable benefits through the change and, when reconciled, to assist in the development of an action

---

[94] Beutler, L. Storm, A., Kirkish, P., Scogin, F., & Gaines, J. (1985). Parameters in the prediction of police
officer performance. *Professional Psychology: Research and Practice, 16*(2), 324-335.
[95] Chandler, E. & Jones, C. (1979). "Cynicism: An inevitability of police work?" Journal of Police Science and Administration, 7(1), 65-68.

[96] Abbot, 1981 Abbot, T. E. (1986). "The MMPI R-S scale as an indicator of the future development of a cynicism in police applicants." In James Reese and Harvey Goldstein's Psychological Services for Law Enforcement. National Symposium on Police Psychological Services, Washington, D.C., 3-9.

plan. Providing a vision that leads to seeing ways to reward oneself with the new changes often lessens the stress of change. Emotional and social support is helpful as people begin to consider that change is positive and that with planning and attitude whatever is coming will be accepted and adapted to much easier.

What is your role as a coach?

1. Primarily, your role is to provide support, feedback and help with new skills that are needed to address a need.

2. Your role and direct attention to future events is important. While negative events might never occur, should they happen, it will be important to be ready. They are:

- Mission – what is the purpose behind the training and planning?

- Establish a vision, what you want the planning to achieve in the future.

- List the values that are important in the coaching and mentoring training, those adaptations that are important to the individual.

- Who is responsible, how is that determined, how do they insure that responsibility is upheld and understood?

- Who is accountable and how is that determined? Why is accountability important and what happens if it should fail?

Heart of Coaching & Motivation.

When coaching employees or others we have some responsibility to the fact that we are not operating solo. We are teaching, guiding, representing, illustrating and recommending appropriate goals and behaviors we should all follow.

- Lead from the front
- Focus on the whole person
- Mutual trust between parties
- Honest feedback and confidence
- Accountability by all employees
- Strengthen alliances & partnerships
- Confidentiality of another person's issues
- Achieve organization's mission and goals
- Establishing a unique relationship of respect.

Skills needed to be an effective Coach.

Many of these indicators reflect our values, how we see and deal with the world and other people. They are learned behaviors and attitudes and for any person who supervises others, this list is an invaluable set of indicators of our personal competence.

- Write incident reports.
- Communicate with others.

- Know your people.
- Be sincere, maintain eye contact, speak clearly, and listen to the person.
- Trust and have confidence in the coach.
- Coach is invested in doing the right thing.
- Do not attack the person. Support and help bring about change.
- Passion and motivation for what you do.
- Incident driven (usually) – take steps before a crisis hits.
- Straightforward, do not pull punches.
- Respect self and others.
- Fair and consistent.
- Practice what you preach.
- Admit mistakes and move forward.
- Hold self and others accountable.
- Inspire people to do a good job.
- Be sincere in your approach to employees.
- Seek balance with DOC's mission and goals and employee capabilities.
- Be aware of dual agendas (organization and employee).
- Willing to put yourself forward in discussion and not appear disinterested.
- Build on positives and not dwell on negatives.
- Look forward to improvement and success.
- Do not leave coaching session with employee feeling discouraged.
- Follow-up and support the employee along the way as he/she changes.
- Know personalities of the people you supervise and manage.
- Change is difficult, help people with the transition.
- Give frequent feedback, if needed. Remain engaged.

Coaching Defined.

Not all of the indicators listed must be put into play at once. They represent a tool box that, when filled, is of value to both the coach and the person he or she is working with. We must be able to select what works for us, apply it and determine the success of the outcomes.

1. Truthfulness
2. Confidentiality
3. Establishing trust
4. Asking good questions, being curious
5. Proving feedback, support & new skills
6. Creating an alliance and a partnership
7. Willingness to focus on the whole person
8. A relationship that is dynamic and ongoing
9. Being ethical and demonstrating integrity
10. Requesting the person take certain actions
11. Provide increased awareness and information.
12. Place to deal with frustration and anger and fears.
13. A tool for assisting people with the change process.
14. Provide opportunity for someone to express their negative emotions.
15. Focuses on where individuals are not where we would like them to be.

Time and Commitment.

In today's rushed and rushing world, when you are attempting to help someone with behavior or performance and you are in a coaching role, take time and do it right. There are a lot of skills that come to bear and listening and asking the right questions, does not happen with assurance of success, if you rush in your efforts.

1. Schedule appointments and be there. Do not cancel.

2. Meet in a quiet place, post a sign not to be disturbed and make the environment comfortable. No phones ringing, pagers going off, cell phones ringing, for either party.

3. Take notes, insure the individual of confidentiality (secure your notes and keep from telling others).

4. Write out list of steps that will be taken to repair the problem. Have both parties sign after agreement, and establish a follow-up plan.

5. If help is needed, establish the rules by which the employee can call you or engage with other services available to them.

Coaching is useful to help an employee, peer or colleague to overcome demons that may plague them, causing the individual to be off balance with their expectations at work. Stress, adversity and trauma, as we have discussed, is dangerous to the health and welfare of an individual. When we are willing to step in and help, to provide reinforcement and to work out negative influences that contribute to individual dysfunction, then a return to improved health, mental and emotional well-being and improved attitude, engagement and performance on the job will have a greater chance of occurring. Isn't it worth the effort?

Relegating the Unimportant to the Back of the Line.

Spending time on unnecessary tasks does not help with effectiveness or efficiency. We often treat everything on our "To Do" list as equally important. In that matrix, which lacks the simplicity of prioritizing, we do not accomplish efficiency nor are we sorting out those items that are more important than others. This results in inefficiency. This most often results in personal stress and internal pressure that leads to frustration, dysfunction, and loss of patience. All of this can be avoided with a few simple, yet effective tools.

It starts and stops with ourselves! Once we have mastered the fine art of time management, which requires, we are in a place to help others. There are numerous models of time management in existence, pointing to technology, systems, mapping programs and other suggested ways to better manage and be in charge of one's time. As is true in most areas of life, a simple approach to time management is always the most effective!

<u>Pencil and paper or technology.</u> This is a personal decision based on preference and what is known and available to the individual. Lists will be kept, perhaps categorized and a place for notes on status.

- Set up clear categories that will allow for ease in prioritizing and tracking.

- Categories might include "urgent" – "important" – "Can wait," with due dates.

- In coaching or supervising multiple people, keeping separate pages or 'files' for each individual is important. If you are also charged with submitting evaluation reports on individuals, a written record becomes invaluable, particularly if you are keeping track of concerns, plans and progress ongoing.

- A "punch list" of urgent and short-term work can also be kept. These are the things that need immediate attention and things that can be completed without affecting others.

The key is to find a method of organizing your time in a manner that allows you to be effective and efficient in completing your duties. You do not want every moment filled with concern about things that have to be done, not meeting deadlines, and feeling under constant pressure because of the confusion. Establishing a method to manage your time and job duties, sooner rather than later, will become automatic and allow control over addressing the details inherent in this level of work and responsibility. . This reduces stress and improves outlook, use of time, attitude and proficiency.

Chapter 16
Work in Your Sphere of Influence to Assist Others

Introduction.

One of the underlying assumptions of this book is that we owe fellow colleagues respect and a willingness to engage with them in mutual welfare. Mutual welfare is helping someone address, reconcile or overcome issues that are troubling and causing the person to feel stress or other emotional responses that are not deemed healthy or appropriate (e.g., an angry outburst). When we are troubled, work, family relations, social engagement and personal mental and physiological well–being is often harmed. Going it alone, while trying to work through the issue may work, but often it doesn't. Continued irritants eventually affect work performance which may ring potentially negative organizational attention.

We have previously used peer coaching as an approach for managing those identified employees experiencing negative symptoms of stress, adversity and/or trauma. Those concepts are formative in helping a fellow employee. Shana Johnson (2011)[97] provides us with information that helps people feeling isolated at work to successfully work through those feelings.   When we personally feel disconnected from our work place, it is difficult to focus and carry out the normal daily work requirements with positive energy and focus. The things that plague us have a habit of rising to the surface at the most inopportune time, causing disruption, distractedness, and other negative manifestations. Whatever one's role, being uncomfortable and out of place at work is a lonely feeling, puts us on guard, causes suspicion and removes energy from job performance.   Our minds are very accommodating and will take a negative thought or feeling and carry it forward into new realms of consideration that might well exacerbate the negativity–––, at least in one's own head!

As an example, if you genuinely believe your supervisor is not being honest with you and that there is a lack of open communication, you begin to wonder if things are not being withheld from you. You begin to feel angrier at your supervisor, over time; because you are sure that your supervisor has it in for you. Logic tells us that this situation won't improve unless there is some form of communication—an

---

[97] . Johnson, S. (2011). Here is a Way Development & Aid Workers Can Overcome Isolation at Work. http://developmentcrossroads.com/2011/10/here-is-a-way-development-aid-workers-can-overcome-isolation-at-work/

opportunity for the employee to share their genuine feelings with the supervisor in a non-threatening environment. But, that is difficult to do for a number of reasons. There are both valid and incorrect assumptions taking place and unless rationally addressed, they never seem to get better.

Let's take this example a step further along its natural path. This same person, in his feeling of isolation, decides to take his or her concern to their spouse, a family member, or friend outside of the workplace. But how can an 'outsider' truly understand and support this individual? Perhaps the spouse or friend has heard this concern again and again, growing tired and less able to support this individual.

We all know that it is the "inside" discussion that is really the right direction to proceed in, but, how does this employee get there? This is a frequently asked question in search of an appropriate answer.

Solutions may be elusive, but must be sought and found, nonetheless. Pathways to solutions are needed, ones that are sustainable, appropriate and that help restore balance and harmony, thereby removing the employee's feelings of isolation (in this example).

Now we return back to the concept of peer coaching. To review: A peer coach is someone who listens well, gives honest feedback, is trustworthy, sincere, and knows the environment and culture. A peer coach also has to know of his or her limitations and when to refer to someone outside of the organization (such as a licensed therapist), when the employees needs exceed their skill level. A peer coach is knowledgeable of what the person job role and responsibilities are. He or she is someone with a similar level of work experience, and who is familiar with the organization and work culture of the employee.

Peer coaches address a variety of issues regarding stress, difficult situations regarding work performance and/or with one's boss, career issues or personal concerns, among other things. Caution is urged when moving too far beyond the employees work environment and/or performance, however.

Johnson (2011[98]) offers the following relationship conditions to be a successful peer coach or, even more realistically, to be of help to someone at the worksite.

1. The coach will always keep conversations confidential.
2. The coach and employee can trust each other to be honest in terms of sharing problems and providing a reality check, as needed
3. Coaches are good listeners and do not emphasize their personal ideas, advice or agenda.
4. Coaches understand the work context and environment.
5. Coaches are able to share aloud and manage personality so as not to engage in power plays.

---

[98] Johnson, S. (2011). Here is a Way Development & Aid Workers Can Overcome Isolation at Work. http://developmentcrossroads.com/2011/10/here-is-a-way-development-aid-workers-can-overcome-isolation-at-work/

<u>Recognizing symptoms & situations.</u>

The purpose of establishing programs for employees who may be experiencing stress, adversity or trauma is to minimize problems and maximize performance. Attitude, motivation, problems, actions and employee well-being are also components of the decision-making process. Knowing what to look for and when to intervene is important for good decision-making and to maintain a positive employment environment. To that end, Lumb & Breazeale (2008)[99] offer the following goals to facilitate change within the individual and the organizational culture. They include:

- Identify and develop intervention strategies to counter employee attitudes and behaviors that hinder or impede the implementation of programs by police agencies that change historic practices.

- Facilitate employee acceptance of and integration into a changing organization that embraces service delivery, employees, and quality of life of the community.

- Encourage an environment of trust, cooperation, and communications among individuals across the organization.

- Determine employee perceptions of issues and needs utilizing a survey instrument. Focusing on the needs of the department and its employees reduces dissention, tension, problems and assists employee in assuming a more inclusive and participatory position.

- Develop and implement continuing professional development programs designed to facilitate the fulfillment of the organization's mission and goals.

- Enhance supervisor effectiveness helping them improve their coaching skills and abilities related to employee performance issues and facilitate the line officers role as problem solvers in the community.

- Train supervisors to address the primary causes of employee performance problems in such a way as to increase the officer's empathy and effectiveness in addressing these problems when they encounter them in the community they serve.

The anticipated benefits of a peer coaching program include the following:

---

[99] Lumb, R., & Breazeale, R. (2008). Peer Coaching: Managing Police Culture. A manuscript for a train-the-trainer program. Copyright at Wilton, Maine.

- Reduce complaints.

- Improve employee performance and participation in achieving agency mission, goals and values.

- Provide supervisors and management with skills and knowledge to address issues and problems of citizen trust and respect, strengthen services to the community, reduce misconduct, and resolve individual problems of negative attitude and behavior.

- Encourage and build an environment of optimism and good will among employees and with the community.

<u>Making a Decision: To Seek Employee Engagement or Not.</u>

Employee Assistance Programs (EAP) has existed for a long time. Unfortunately, public service agency employees do not utilize them to their advantage. All too frequently seeking emotional or mental health assistance is often seen as a personal weakness, as what is troubling the individual is often considered to be "only temporary." Many problems encountered at work are not related to the employment; rather they emerge from substance abuse, family problems, financial issues, and/or mental health issues.

There is a corresponding cost to the organization in lost productivity, increased sick leave, low motivation, burnout, accidents, grievances, turnover, low job satisfaction, mistakes, and other issues that affect the quality of work and outcomes. These issues become extremely concerning given the nature of the work and the accompanying accountability and responsibility. The cost for related issues runs into the billions of dollars nationally.

From awareness to action, there is generally a substantial period of time displacement. Frequently, the passage of time does not cure the issue. Indeed, it actually may exacerbate the issue, taking what might have been an easy fix, to a more complicated and serious level. Often when someone finally reaches that level of self-destruction, it becomes public knowledge, and the individual faces suspension, firing or prosecution. These are all costly and generally unnecessary outcomes, if the situation had been acted on earlier. We expect that supervisors do their job to inquire as to the issue or problem facing the individual, engaging them in conversation or offering some level of support or intervention. But in reality, that does not happen as often as it should. The decision to act requires action based on facts, a plan to address the needs and issues, and a willing employee who will work with the supervisor in finding solutions.

Lumb, et al (2009, 10-19)[100], offer information about the peer coaching role. The following information is from that manuscript. It is warranted when employee

---

[100] . Lumb, R., Breazeale, R., Metz, G., & Lumb, P. (2009, Fall). Public Safety Officer Emotional Health: Addressing the Silent Killer. The Correctional Trainer.

behavior and work related performance do not comply with the organization's mission, policy and standards of practice. Deviation from acceptable practice should initiate supervisor action. Success hinges on knowing the employee and a willingness to help by all parties. Identification of problem behavior or performance and making the decision to act is somewhat subjective and includes a broad array of variables and considerations. Decision-making is co-dependent on having solid information and confidence in what must take place.

If we can say with certainty that we want to engage and help, then perhaps it is useful to know some of the intervention tools that can be helpful. Examples of intervention tools would be to refer the troubled employee to an agency for assessment and supportive counseling. Another possibility is to adequately develop a team of employees, overseen by a supervisor, who are thoroughly trained in the peer coaching model to include problem-solving, resilience building, and addressing divisive issues that impact on performance. They would be well versed and able to identify the signs and symptoms when a colleague is heading down the slippery slope toward dysfunction or self-destruction. This team would work with the development and delivery of resiliency training in the work place and serve as the "go to" people within the agency to approach an officer in a supportive manner and provide guidance toward wellness. This will hasten the return to healthy productivity and reduce lost work time and accompanying problems.

We adhere to the principle that "good relationships and coping strategies are the key to success in every area of human activity" (Stein & Book, 2000[101]). To be successful, it is important that the employee is able to know and manage themselves. In policing and public safety, as perhaps with few other occupations, it is necessary that employees are sound, sane, and optimistic about the world they work within. It is incumbent that supervisors and managers are trained to identify the onset of problems and have the requisite skills and knowledge to intervene effectively with the employee.

As such, they must be aware of the many influences that impact on the individual and require corrective action. Partial skills and expertise are not sufficient. The peer coach must be well versed and trained in intervention and follow-up that also includes evaluation and attention to the personality and behavioral characteristics of the individual.

Corrective action addresses employee behavior, performance, and activities that were outside of policy, procedures and rules of conduct. Normally, we take corrective action to punish past behavior and prevent future occurrence. Sometimes this has the desired effect. But, all too often it tends to drive the employee toward a more secretive and low profile position, where caution is exercised, but attitudes and behavior may remain at or below pre-event levels. We sometimes lose trust with lingering disfavor, which then interferes in the workplace by creating even more tension and disruption.

Coaching is not punitive. Instead it seeks to engage the individual in a collaborative process with the supervisor or peers providing assistance. Coaching is about change, helping a person to do better, to drop old habits and to be a more

---

[101] Stein, S.J., and Book, H.E. (2000). *The EQ Edge: Emotional Intelligence and Your Success.* Toronto: Stoddard Publishing.

effective employee. Coaching is done to intervene in work related performance problems, not personal issues. The driving force may be personal but work guidance is focused on performance. The coach strives to help the employee make appropriate life and performance changes and to do so in a positive and non-threatening manner.

Assisting the employee to find resolution to problems and bring about sustainable change in their thinking and behavior involves a guided process and supervisor participation. This is a collaborative process where both parties seek the best method to achieving goals the employee stated as part of setting change goals. The coach assists the employee in conducting a self-assessment, list strengths, and articulate expectations, examine barriers to success and stipulate what motivates them (Whitworth et al., 1998). Motivation includes several aspects of the job and each is a separate target goal. They include:

1. Job Performance
2. Productivity
3. Job Satisfaction
4. Promotion & Advancement
5. Outlook and Attitude

Motivation helps the employee acquire and maintain an enthusiastic attitude while retaining a positive outlook toward their job and the organization. Motivation guides improvement, contributes to work performance, increases engagement with other employees, and reinforces an improved attitude toward the organization. Effective coaching skills provide guidance and help a person by using the coach's own skills, knowledge and experience, applied to the situation or issue being addressed. Coaching another person demands commitment, dedication, and personal investment. Included in being an effective coach are the following skills:

1. Display patience
2. Communicate clearly
3. Be aware of conflicting agendas
4. Inquire to obtain full information
5. Be willing to take on added responsibility
6. Close the coaching session appropriately, encouraging continued inquiry
7. Schedule adequate time to conduct the session
8. Collaborate with the employee to develop goals and change milestones
9. Respect individual confidentiality

The outcome of the effort, if done timely and sincerely, is saving an employee of value, helping someone overcome personal demons, and in the long-run saves money from lost productivity related to negative symptoms of the employee's stress and adversity. And, most importantly, it is the right thing to do!

<u>Summary Statement.</u>

Assisting an individual in acquiring special skills and knowledge that are useful in addressing personal needs and establishing a foundation for acquiring skills as a peer coach is a primary goal of resiliency training. That goal is to help each employee learn to engage in self-monitoring of stressful issues, and with that knowledge, the ability to moderate the outcomes Public safety is a unique occupation that provides critical services to communities.

Employees are subjected to unusual and stressful situations that, over time, accumulate and result in behaviors and performance problems that cannot be left unaddressed. Addressing and reducing the effects of exposure to danger and traumatic events is a common goal of the individual employee and the organization, and demands that steps are taken to strengthen resilience and sharpen methods and skills used to help employees who may become derailed by the challenges they confront.

We should not expect that simply by telling an employee to "straighten out" that he or she will automatically do so, or possess the skills or resiliency to do so. Success for change is highly dependent on the individual and his or her supervisor, along with substantial levels of sincerity, trust and confidence. Finally, there is no more important supervisory role than to care for and guide subordinates. Helping employees maintain a healthy lifestyle benefits family, peers, work, and the health and welfare of the individual. To accomplish this, resilience training provides a great number of benefits to all involved.

Chapter 17
Building a Multi-Layered Community Connection

Introduction.

Research and discussions about police stress and the terrible toll it takes has been raging for decades. Still, we are milling around acting as if it does not exist. We take insufficient notice, are told to suck it up, be tough and get on with the work. Shame on us!

As previously discussed, there is no question that continuous exposure to stress, adversity and trauma results in harm to the individual's emotional, psychological and social well-being. The manifestations include all manner of dysfunction, harm and occasional death. Not only does the first responder suffer, but so, too, do their friends, colleagues, family members and other associates who are often sucked into the morass of problems.

The question is what do we do about it? We cannot continue as we are, can we? I am somewhat pessimistic that change will take place. However, that attitude cannot prevail as it defeats the purpose of this book. So, what is to be done, what transition of mind, attitude, policy and philosophy is needed for change to occur, and how do we get there? It starts with disbursement of the notion that the organization is a collection of separate units and divisions, unequal, specific in nature, and apart by necessity. That very description illustrates what has existed for decades within the realm of police/first responders. The time to seek an alternative solution is now.

1. Why the wagon must be pulled from the front.

When we stop seeing the organization as a collection of individuals who share a common purpose, we self-select into fragmented units. In those units where our reality and loyalty reside we often think, act and support along those narrow lines. This attitude naturally separates us from others, both horizontally and vertically. We tend to disconnect and not retain concern for other component parts, beyond occasional sharing of work related moments.

In reality, the workplace is tightly tied to the whole and extends beyond the actual organization to numerous others including other agencies, family, friends and the larger community. In the parent agency, the need for solidarity, regardless of rank and position, is needed when we are confronting the *effects of harm* on our employees that are related to aspects of the job. In the public- safety and first responder world, those *effects of harm* are potentially present with every response to calls for service. It does not matter if the responder is male or female, what their religion, ethnicity, education, rank, or other variables are, as the effects of exposure to the conditions that elicit stress, adversity or trauma strike without consideration.

The dangers of A.S.A.T. (accumulated stress, adversity and trauma) are not over-emphasized: they are very real. Why then would we consider separate solutions to a common problem? The new officer, now high ranking and with twenty-five years under his or her belt, carries the same levels and experiences of stress, accumulated over the years, as the officer with three to five years of experience. There are, of course, varying degrees of depth and effect. But, the point is-, there is relevance in the common issues. However, the solutions are not being addressed. I It is important to identify the enemy, formulate a plan of attack and get to it as the organization joins together to formulate a plan that involves pulling the problem "wagon" from the front—the united front!

2. The employee is the focus.

Employees represent the organization and as such, they are often the single contact whose performance and behavior represent the services provided. Hiring, training and allowing the employee to represent the organization are costly and critically necessary steps. If the job they will do includes exposure to frequent stress, adversity and trauma, it is important to minimize the potential harm it can bring. It would seem that when a common problem such as S.A.T. is confronted by all employees, regardless of position, in common agreement and with a sustained united front, good things can and do happen. This is one area where solidarity is essential. Displacement of rational planning and action should be avoided. The agency head should establish a working group consisting of employees from all levels of the agency, including sworn/licensed, certified and civilian members. The purpose is to discuss the issues, research solutions, design and implement policy and programs that will address the problems related to S.A.T that will result sustainable solutions.

The working group must have employees from all segments of the agency for it to be representative of all people and their unique exposure to S.A.T. For example, while patrol officers are on the front line to those conditions that generate stress, those who have gone before carry the outcomes of similar exposure with their time at the front, as well. Dispatchers, support staff, supervisors, administrators and all others within the organization each have their stories to tell and all must be engaged in finding solutions.

Collaboration, exploration, drilling down into the root causes and contributors to the problem being addressed is a step that cannot be ignored or skipped. We cannot make informed decisions without information. The planning process must be thorough, comprehensive, informed and result in a tight and fully vetted program whose effectiveness meets desired outcomes. The actual process for employees to access a program or programs where the desired help is found, must be simple, confidential, and demonstrate its effectiveness in a consistent manner.

Hosting Information Sessions:

With a program as important as this discussion indicates, we must strive for 100 percent inclusiveness for employees. Meetings that focus on discussion will provide the information that is desired. Employees must feel part of what is taking place and choose to participate. If there is some concern about confidentiality, having one individual represent many and bringing the collective comments to the table, is often an acceptable approach. For example, The Tallahassee, FL, Police Department held Vertical Staff Meetings that were attended by people representing all segments of the agency. This removed the concern for voicing one's personal issues as it blended into a diverse yet equal and unified focus. Information gathered in these sessions was recorded and used in planning positive change. If tasks were forthcoming, there was follow-up with all participating members receiving full information.

The Planning Process:

Awareness of the problem is step one. Gathering information (drilling down to bedrock—step two) brings about full understanding. Acknowledgement that the problem (or concern) is shared by the majority of all employees is step three. And then we must use that knowledge for a purposeful program (step four). This is the planning process in a nutshell. It, too, must be thorough, fully informed, have a mission, vision, values and goals foundation, leading to - ease of application and effective programs that employees can choose from.

Planning will take time. A planning model is needed and adherence to each step important. Skipping seemingly unimportant aspects might well ignore what will, in the end, be critical. Deeply discuss and explore to gain depth of understanding. Put all scenarios on the table and use that knowledge to build foundation and comprehensiveness.

FEMA offers a variety of planning processes to address the mitigation of hazards that might emerge from natural or manmade disasters[102]. As an example, the following five step process has relevance to the adverse effects of S.A.T. I would note that I see "hazards" in the same light as S.A.T., as over the long haul it is as deadly to your health and well-being.

1. Establish goals and objectives aimed at reducing or avoiding vulnerabilities to the identified hazards;

2. Identify actions that will help you accomplish the established goals;

3. Set forth strategies that detail how the mitigation actions will be implemented and administered.

4. Provide continuity to the planning process as it provides a link between determining what your community's risks are and actually implementing mitigation actions; and

5. Establish a process for regular updates and review of the plan.

Establishing goals and strategies is very important, a must, and certainly establishes a mindset worth adopting.

Community Capacity - The Other Variable:

---

[102] . http://www.fema.gov/plan-prepare-mitigate

The Aspen Institute[103], in their publication "Measuring Community Capacity Building" states: "*Community capacity is the combined influence of a community's commitment, resources and skills that can be deployed to build on community strengths and address community problems and opportunities.*" This applies to the topic at hand when we accept that employees are a community. In their description they allude to the importance of heightened support to address problem solving and strengthening the community of interest. How could that not be positive?

Coupled with the will to achieve and sustain solutions, there is also the need for resources to be available including financial, human and other types of support. The skills, knowledge and abilities of employees, when coupled with their expertise and experience, are a powerful factor in the likely success of the planning process. Strengthening the capacity of the organization takes place by degrees, sometimes fast and sometimes slowly, but ever progressing forward toward the desired goals.

More importantly, all efforts are meaningless unless we measure process and outcomes. Jumping into a process and not looking at results as we progress is quite common and very foolish. We must be able to identify when something is not working and fix it or make adjustments. To do otherwise is generally a waste of time and effort. Community capacity is enhanced when we are committed to the task, have adequate resources to get the job done, and have the right people working on the project.

Community capacity building, in this case to devise and develop a program to address the negative effects of S.A.T. is dependent on motivation and enthusiasm for the task. Leadership must be present, desire to achieve the goals and needs identified as high priority, establish and maintain strong commitment, and more importantly, work to shape the future. It should be said that it is not just an internal effort, for the larger community must be included as well. There are community stakeholders who can help and who would be more than willing, if approached and asked. Their inclusion could have a powerful influence on the overall outcome.

Communities and the people that live in them need to take responsibility for problems that exist, to the extent possible and appropriate. Successful problem-solving elicits local wisdom and knowledge, aspects of history and the communities desire to improve and represent positive quality of life. These same reasons fit within police and public safety agencies when an issue or problem becomes known. Addressing solutions is easier when there is a process that guides people toward sustainable solutions.

Who in the Community Can Help?

1. Professional services such as Employee Assistance Programs.
2. Private providers of mental health services.
3. Trained Peer reviewers.

---

[103]. ASPEN Institute/Rural Economic Policy Program, Measuring Community Capacity Building. Ver. 3/96.

<u>Summary Statement</u>.

The organization must be a collection of individuals with a common purpose, goals, and willing compliance to the mission, vision, values and goals. Employees must feel part of what is taking place and choose to participate. As a community of people, we tend to care for one another, to be aware of issues that can be addressed, to offer a helping hand when needed, and through solidarity, seek to improve the work environment.

Addressing solutions is easier when there is a process that guides people toward sustainable solutions, versus clinging tightly to problems and rehashing them over and over again with no positive solutions or change in sight. Employees and management must take responsibility for identified problems and make every attempt to solve them. The collective is stronger than the individuals, as pulling the wagon together certainly makes the job easier and the outcomes more assured.

A healthy organization considers itself a family of individuals who all share in the success and desired outcomes for which they exist. I speak of attitude and the need to address problems, seek solutions and move forward without harboring dissention, anger and negative feelings.

Precluding harm to our employees is a primary goal of the organization. We share in the good and the bad, we rejoice when it is appropriate, and we feel the sadness of others and at the end of the day. As such we must share responsibility for one another and importantly the organization. It provides our home away from home, it is the glue that forms the brotherhood of common duty and mission, and we can gain sustenance if we reduce the animosity. Keep the inside strong for it weakens the work if energy is constantly diverted to issues.

Stress, adversity and trauma are harmful. There is sufficient cause of its presence due to the work that is done; it should not be the result of internal strife and disharmony. From the Chief of CEO to the newest employee, the message is the same, make it work! Find solutions before the issues overwhelm. Address problems when they are known and take wide consideration of the employees and their needs, as well as others with whom the agency provides service. Solidarity is not blind, it is flexible, it is concerned for the whole and it works to improve, not destroy. Policy, procedures, programs and concerned employees is powerful glue that can hold it all together.

APPENDIX A.

From chapter 6 – Increasing Employee Self-Control. Self-Assessment.

<u>Instructions</u>: For each statement below circle your response

SA = Strongly Agree, **A** = Agree, **U** = Undecided, **D** = Disagree, **SD** = Strongly Disagree

1	When opportunities exist for employees to work independently (without supervision) there will be an increase in efficiency	SA A U D SD
2	Although attempts are made at giving employees more responsibility, they will seldom use these opportunities.	SA A U D SD
3	Employees, on their own, will in most cases do what is required of them.	SA A U D SD
4	Employees should be given more opportunities to determine their tasks to be accomplished.	SA A U D SD
5	Strict controls in organizations are required for efficient operation.	SA A U D SD
6	Employee participation in decision-making produces greater harmony between supervisor and employee.	SA A U D SD
7	More responsibility given to employees will result in benefits to the individual employee and the organization.	SA A U D SD
8	Allowing employees to manage their own personal leave time (sick, vacation, personal business, etc.) will result in abuse.	SA A U D SD
9	Allowing more employee initiative in the work place would cause much confusion.	SA A U D SD
10	Participative decision-making is of little value because most subordinates do not understand the overall objective of the organization.	SA A U D SD
11	When employees are given more responsibility in the work environment, they will be more committed to the organizations goals and objectives.	SA A U D SD
12	Allowing employees to start work anytime they desire (within a two-hour flexible range), where possible, will result in confusion and inefficiency	SA A U D SD
13	When left on their own most subordinates will not do the work that is required of them.	SA A U D SD
14	Employees who are committed to organizational goals and objectives require little supervision.	SA A U D SD
15	Given the opportunity, most employees will make decisions that benefit the organization and the employees.	SA A U D SD
16	Most employees are unable to identify with the organization or its objectives.	SA A U D SD

Scoring sheet.

Increasing Employee Self-Control Scoring Sheet

<u>Instructions</u>: Circle the response you gave to each item. Sum all circled numbers under each column (SA, A, U, D, and SD), and then sum across all columns for a total score.

	SA	A	U	D	SD
1	5	4	3	2	1
2	1	2	3	4	5
3	5	4	3	2	1
4	5	4	3	2	1
5	1	2	3	4	5
6	5	4	3	2	1
7	5	4	3	2	1
8	1	2	3	4	5
9	1	2	3	4	5
10	1	2	3	4	5
11	5	4	3	2	1
12	1	2	3	4	5
13	1	2	3	4	5
14	5	4	3	2	1
15	5	4	3	2	1
16	1	2	3	4	5
Sub-Total					

Total Score: _____

IFSC Interpretation

Place an "X" on the continuum below to indicate the degree to which you are in favor or increasing employee self-control and self-determination. For example, scores of 16–24 indicated that you are definitely not in favor of having employees manage their own organizational contingencies, have more responsibility, and participate more in decision making.

A continuum of Attitudes toward Increasing Employee Self Control

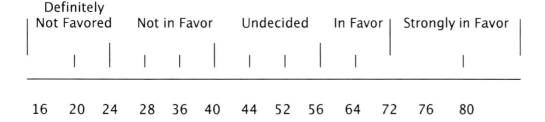

APPENDIX B

THE MOFFATTS LYRICS

"You Are What You Do"

Coulda been my grandpa, coulda been my preacher
Coulda been my third grade history teacher
Somebody said it and I'll never forget it
Mighta been my daddy, mighta been my mama
Mighta been Dolly Parton or the Dalai Lama
They were words to the wise
And they hit me right between the eyes

If you wanna write a song, better get a guitar
If you wanna win Daytona, better get you a car
If you wanna be Picasso, better get you some paint

Son, you are what you do
And if you don't, then you ain't
Coulda been a stranger, coulda been a friend
Coulda been a commentator on CNN
Talkin' through my TV directly to me
Mighta been my butcher, mighta been my baker
Mighta been an outta work undertaker down at the Superette
Who gave me this reality check

If you wanna go to heaven, you better go to church
If you wanna promotion, you better get to work
If you wanna catch the big one, better get you some bait
Yeah, you are what you do
And if you don't then you ain't
If you want an education, you better stay in school

Get some sunglasses if you wanna be cool
Talk to Mother Teresa if you wanna be a saint
Yeah, you are what you do
And if you don't, then you ain't
Yeah, you are what you do
And if you don't then you ain't

Made in the USA
Middletown, DE
18 March 2018